COMPUTING
FOR BEGINNERS

get the most from your computer

THIRD
EDITION

★★

VALERIE SHERMAN

Acknowledgements
p.2 © Julien Grondin/Istock; p. 5 © Romain Diant/ Fotolia.

First published in 2002

Second revised edition published in 2004 as *Getting the Most from your Computer.*

This third revised edition published in 2008 by Age Concern Books
1268 London Road, London, SW16 4ER, United Kingdom.

ISBN-13: 978–0–86242–439-8

A catalogue record for this book is available from the British Library.

Edited by Sarah Price.

Typeset by GreenGate Publishing Services, Tonbridge, Kent.

Printed in Great Britain by Latimer Trend, Plymouth, Devon.

About the author

Jackie Sherman is currently teaching IT to adults in the community. She also writes computer course materials for distance learning colleges and answers IT queries for various websites and magazines aimed at people over 50.

Jackie graduated in Zoology from Oxford University and worked for the British Council in Ethiopia. She then joined the CBI to work in its education department, before spending 12 years as a university careers adviser. After training as a school teacher, she became involved with several educational research projects before moving into adult basic skills and computers.

Acknowledgements

To Graham, William, Toby and Beryl for all their support.

Contents

Using this book

This book will enable you to enjoy your computer more and save time when using it. Books can never take the place of a personal tutor, and so the ideal is to find a local IT class that you can attend to get you started. This book can then be used to support and extend your learning, as well as for reference if you get stuck trying to carry out an activity on your own at home.

It is likely that many of you reading this book will not be completely new to computers. Research shows that it is incorrect to assume that most people who are over 50 and interested in learning about computers have never used one. You may well have used a computer at work, perhaps gaining some experience of a particular software package, or you may have observed children, grandchildren or other relatives using one at home. You may even have bought a computer but not yet learned how to use it fully.

It is hoped that this book will be especially valuable for those of you in this situation. Not only will it introduce you to the basic aspects of applications you may not have come across before, but it will also show you how to develop your skills and use the more interesting features of familiar software packages. You will also be shown how to make use of the integrated aspects of computer programs, for example, copying drawings or charts produced in one package to another package to improve the quality of your documents, or attaching them to emails so that you can share them with other people.

Each chapter looks at one of the main uses for a computer and takes you through an introduction to the basic skills required before moving on to useful and enjoyable projects such as creating greetings cards, attaching files to emails, playing games with others on the internet or producing charts.

The detailed instructions are based on PCs running Windows XP as the operating system and using the software suite Microsoft Office XP (2002), which includes Word for word processing, Excel for spreadsheets and PowerPoint for presentations. There are so many similarities between these and slightly earlier or later versions that you should find it quite straightforward to use the information in this book even if you have Microsoft Office 2000 or 2003, or are running Windows 98, ME or 2000.

Most of the menus and commands that are in these applications are very similar to those in Microsoft Office XP.

A glossary is provided to explain technical terms and there is an index at the end to help you find your way around the book. Each of the main chapters ends with suggestions for simple tasks to help you practice many of the skills covered in the book.

Once you have mastered all these skills you should feel confident enough to move on to the accompanying level 2 book: *Everyday Computing: Improve your Skills in Easy Steps*.

All menu options and buttons are shown in **bold type**. When you see entries such as **File – Save** it means open the **File** menu and then click the **Save** option.

Introduction: Why bother with computers?

Computers are not only for the young, nor are they a luxury that older people can well do without. People over 50, whether they are retired or not, have a wide range of interests and **Information Technology (IT)** can help in many ways, including the following:

- If you are involved with any local clubs or societies, or you give the occasional talk, you can use your computer. For example, you can build up a database of members' names and addresses; produce documents, such as programmes or newsletters; and simplify sending letters out using the envelope or label facilities. You can also create professional-looking documents, charts, slides or even computerised presentations.

- If you are housebound or find it hard to meet people, yet want to make contact with others having similar interests and hobbies – or if you simply want to keep in touch with friends and family – you can register for an email address so that you can send your messages electronically, or you can use chat rooms and newsgroups to pick up useful hints or exchange ideas. You can even play games online with other people.

- Should you find shopping too tiring, you can browse the 'virtual' aisles of online supermarkets, select goods and organise home delivery via the internet. You can also check out the cheapest prices by comparing different retailers' offers before buying almost anything online.

- If you want to save money and be creative at the same time, you can make your own greetings cards or headed paper, for example.

- You can learn something new – take a course online, or buy a do-it-yourself CD-ROM, on a topic such as interior design or garden planning.

- If you want to sell things or advertise your services, it is quite easy to use your computer to produce advertisements, posters or flyers, as well as put items into an online auction.

- For anyone who likes music, it is simple to 'download' songs or sheet music from the internet, listen to recordings before you buy or simply read reviews in online magazines and newspapers.

- If you miss a favourite radio or television programme, you can even use your computer to catch up with a 'podcast' or 'vodcast'.

- Finding information on anything from train timetables to hotels, art exhibitions, local evening classes, the weather, recipes, knitting patterns, films or spare parts for your lawnmower is so easy with a computer – you just need to **surf** the world wide web.

Will it be difficult?

When you haven't learnt anything new for a while, or don't feel you are particularly good with 'machines', you may worry that computers are going to be too difficult or technical to master. Yet adult education classes are full of mature students happily getting to grips with word processing or surfing the world wide web and sending emails. It is clear from the numbers of older people attending computing classes that age is not a problem. Some of the fastest, most enthusiastic and successful learners are in their 50s and 60s, or older. Good learners, however, do seem to have certain characteristics in common:

- they feel able to make mistakes and learn from them

- they are willing to read and follow instructions

- they are prepared to 'have a go'

- they are quite content to learn at their own pace and take things a step at a time.

Although it can slow you down if you forget what you did last week, you don't have to have a good memory to succeed with computers. Keeping your own notes, referring to books and getting help from the computer itself, via the help menus, all mean that you don't need to worry too much if you forget how to carry out a particular task. In most of the software applications you can even find out which button does what by resting the mouse pointer on the button and waiting for the description (known as a **screen tip**) to appear.

What you do need with any new skill is patience, and as older people often have this in abundance, there is no reason at all why anyone who wants to cannot learn to use a computer in a wide variety of ways.

What if you are disabled?

There are various pieces of equipment you can buy or get for free to overcome specific problems when working with your computer, including:

- foot and wrist rests
- shaped keyboards
- document holders
- writing 'pens' or joystick controls
- ergonomic seating
- stands to alter the computer height
- magnifiers to increase the size of everything viewed on the screen
- voice recognition software that allows you to talk rather than type
- speech synthesisers so that text can be 'read aloud' for people who have a visual impairment, or it can be presented in Braille
- special keyboards or mice that can be operated with very limited hand or body movements or even replaced by a switch.

Within the various software applications, you can increase the size of the text display or build up a range of words or phrases that can be inserted automatically, and you can even alter the speeds of mouse or keyboard strokes.

Windows XP provides Accessibility options via the **Start – All Programs – Accessories** menu that allow you to customise your computer to suit your specific needs (by using the Accessibility Wizard) or offer facilities such as a screen magnifier or the Narrator application that will read text out aloud.

More information on adapting your computer can be found on the Microsoft Accessibility website at:

www.microsoft.com/enable

An alternative is to contact a specialist organisation. For blind computer users, the Royal National Institute for Blind People (RNIB) can be found at:

http://www.rnib.org.uk

You can also contact the RNIB by post at:

105 Judd Street
London WC1H 9NE
telephone: 0870 013 9555;
email: technology@rnib.org.uk

The RNIB offers advice on equipment that will make life easier and produces various factsheets on different aspects of working with a computer that are very helpful.

For general advice, you can also contact the charity The Ability Net, which can be found at:

www.abilitynet.org.uk

You an also contact The Ability Net by post at:

PO Box 94
Warwick
Warwickshire CV34 5WS

telephone: 0800 269545;
email: enquiries@abilitynet.org.uk

The Ability Net advises on the wealth of hardware and software solutions – known as 'adaptive' or 'alternative' technologies – now available to overcome any difficulties you may have.

How much will it cost?

If you haven't got your own computer and are thinking of buying one, a new computer for home use that can link to the internet and run any of the software applications you are likely to use will cost between £500 and £1,000 at the time of writing. For this, you should get good sound and image quality, enough memory for running applications, a large capacity hard drive for storing applications and files, and a basic printer. Many retailers also include a 'bundle' of software packages, although not necessarily Microsoft Office.

It starts to become more expensive if you want to use other hardware items such as:

- a digital camera to convert your own photographs into computer files;

- a scanner to copy book or magazine pages into the machine;

- advanced colour or laser printers; or

- a portable MP3 player (see page 126) to play music downloaded from the internet.

To check out the best prices, you could consult the latest *Which?* consumer guides in your local library, or buy one of the many PC magazines aimed at new computer users. A good one is *ComputerActive* as it comes out fortnightly and is written in 'plain English'.

Buying a computer

This is now something many people do via the internet – you can use retailer sites to find out about deals but still use the telephone to place your order, or you can complete an order form and buy directly online. If you are not ready to do this, there are a number of high street stores that offer special deals, such as Argos, Currys Digital, Toys 'R' Us, PC World and even on occasion supermarkets such as Tesco. You may prefer to buy a computer magazine in the newsagents and send for catalogues from computer manufacturers or specialist retailers, such as Dell or Evesham.

Although you can find second-hand computers advertised in local newspapers or online, they may not turn out to be economical in the longer term as their smaller memory and slower processing speed may prevent you making the most of today's software applications. Technology moves on so fast that you should also check that there is room to add further memory or extra hardware so that you can upgrade your computer when you need to.

Saving money

Once you start work, the main ongoing expenses will be paper for the pages you print, ink cartridges for your printer and telephone or service charges when you connect to the internet. In Chapter 8 you will find tips on keeping internet phone charges low, and once you start creating your own headed paper, greetings cards or leaflets you can begin to see that computers could save you quite a bit of money. When you add to this a free 'yellow pages' service so that you can look up any business address or telephone number; not having to buy any more stamps and envelopes when sending your mail electronically; reading newspapers and magazines online; being able to use the internet to compare prices and buy the cheapest holidays, theatre tickets or cars; and the availability of free tutorials on a range of subjects, you may wonder why you didn't start using a computer years ago.

Other options

If you aren't interested in owning a computer, there are places you can go to use equipment cheaply or for free. Check your local community groups, college, library or post office facilities, or call in to an internet or cyber café where you can use a computer for a few pounds an hour and get a coffee at the same time.

Working with a computer

There is a great deal of jargon surrounding IT and using a computer can be confusing when you are on your own. This chapter explains the basic facts about computers and introduces you to some of the technical terms you will meet later in the book. It covers:

- hardware and software
- parts of the computer
- other equipment
- caring for your computer
- your health and safety
- the desktop (including using the mouse, the Start menu, turning the machine on and off and changing the settings)
- working with windows.

Hardware and software

At its simplest, **hardware** refers to parts of the computer you can see and touch, such as the screen, cables, printer or mouse. **Software** is the name given to any instructions, in the form of **programs**, that the computer needs to be able to work effectively.

Software can be stored in different places:

- inside your computer on the main disk (referred to as the hard disk or (C:) drive);
- on floppy disks which are inserted into the 3½-inch floppy (A:) drive (these are only now found on older computers); or
- on CDs that are placed on the slide-out tray in the (D:) drive.

There are two main types of software:

- **Systems** software – which includes the operating system (such as Microsoft Windows) and programs controlling your hardware (for example, the mouse or printer). Most systems software is already present when you buy your computer, so that you can use your mouse or keyboard straightaway, but some may have to be installed; for example, if you want to use a new digital camera.

- **Applications** software – all the programs you use at your computer, such as word processing or drawing packages.

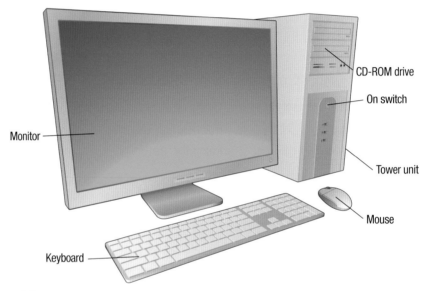

Figure 1.1

Parts of the computer

When you buy a computer, you will always need the basic hardware components: monitor (screen); mouse; desktop or tower unit housing the **Central Processing Unit (CPU)**; memory (**Random Access Memory [RAM]**) and **hard disk**; a **keyboard**; and a **printer** (see Figure 1.1). One alternative is to use a laptop or notebook computer. This is smaller than a PC because it has a built-in screen and mouse, but it works in exactly the same way.

Computer **space** is measured in bytes, kilobytes (KB), megabytes (MB) or gigabytes (GB). If you are buying a computer, you should buy one with the biggest hard disk you can afford, so that there is enough room to store all your programs and **files** (files are the pieces of work, such as word-processed documents, that you create on your computer). Although the minimum requirement is 6 to 10GB, many systems are now supplied with around 40GB.

For the most flexible way of working, you need at least 64 to 128MB of memory (RAM) as this allows you to work with sophisticated programs, carry out different tasks at the same time and speeds up all the activities you are performing.

As with a TV, the size of the screen is down to personal choice but it is probably best to buy one that is at least 17 inches.

Other equipment

Once you become confident using a basic computer system, you can expand it by linking it to other equipment that will allow you to be much more versatile. This could include:

- a digital camera – so that you can view, edit and print out your own photographs

- a scanner – to allow you to turn magazine or book text and pictures into computerised data that you can then incorporate into your own work.

How to get the most from these items of equipment is fully explained in the accompanying level 2 book, *Everyday Computing: Improve your Skills in Easy Steps*.

Caring for your computer

You don't need to worry too much about special precautions for looking after a computer, as normal housekeeping rules apply. In particular, it is sensible to keep food and liquids away from any electrical items; CDs can be badly affected by dirt, heat or magnetism, or become scratched through mishandling.

Unfortunately, when you use the internet or borrow disks, you may introduce rogue programs known as *viruses* that can badly affect your computer. To safeguard your machine, it is a good idea to ask the company that sells you a computer to include anti-virus software, or to buy this software from a company such as Norton or McAfee. You should follow any instructions to update the anti-virus software on a regular basis. Some anti-virus packages are even available free on the internet, such as AVG from **www.grisoft.com**.

3

Your health and safety

One of the major problems with computers is that they are addictive; you can spend hours on the machine without realising it. This can mean sitting in a cramped position straining your back, neck or wrists, or gripping the mouse too tightly for too long a period.

The answer is to set your computer equipment up properly and to do things in moderation. Don't sit for more than 30 minutes at a time before getting up and moving around. Try to hold the mouse lightly, and sit in a chair that supports your back and allows you to keep your eyes roughly level with the monitor and feet comfortably on the floor. Your arms should be level with the keyboard, and everything should be kept close to hand so that you aren't stretching awkwardly to reach the printer or documents you may be working from. If eyestrain or glare is a problem, you could draw the curtains or blinds or reposition the machine; stop working at any sign of a headache or distorted vision.

Most people can work happily with a computer if they take these sensible precautions, but you should always see a doctor or optician if you have persistent problems.

The desktop

With Windows XP, after turning on the power and waiting for the computer to go through its set-up procedure, you will see an opening screen (known as the desktop) that has a coloured or patterned background and a large button, labelled **Start**, in the bottom left-hand corner. One or more small pictures (icons) may be visible, representing common objects in an office, such as a waste paper basket (Recycle Bin), a computer (My Computer) and filing cabinet (My Documents).

Figure 1.2

Using the mouse

To send instructions to your computer, you can use either the keyboard or the mouse. Pressing keys is simple, but the mouse may take a while to master.

The mouse has two buttons on the top. The left button is used to carry out all main activities such as opening documents, adding a tick to a box or selecting objects on the screen.

The right button is only used when you want to display a short menu – a list of relevant options.

In the centre, you often find a wheel. Gently pushing this forward or back with the finger will scroll up and down the screen.

If you roll the mouse gently around on its mat, you will see an arrow-shaped pointer move across the screen. With practice, you will be able to control this movement so that you can rest the pointer on any part of the screen. Press or **click** the left mouse button to make your selection. Selected items usually change colour so that if you click the wrong item by mistake it will be quite clear and you can move the pointer and click again. Even if your clicking opens a window you didn't want to open, just close it (as explained in the section on working with windows on page 10) and try again.

Always click the left mouse button firmly but quickly when opening or selecting items or carrying out the main computer activities. Holding down the left button and then dragging the mouse across the mat will enable you to move objects on the screen or select text word by word.

Your mouse can be used for a number of activities, and the shape of the pointer when you use it determines the specific action. For example:

- Click an arrow and you can select a menu option or add a tick to a box.
- Click a vertical bar over text and you place an insertion point on the screen.
- Click a hand and you open a new page on the world wide web.

When the left mouse button is clicked twice very fast (**double-clicking**), it opens a program or file. (This action can be replaced by one click and then pressing Enter on the keyboard.) In a text document, double-clicking will select a word, and **triple-clicking** (ie three fast clicks) will select a paragraph.

The Start menu

The icons visible on the desktop will vary depending on who first set up the computer. Each one represents a shortcut to a common program/ application or file stored on your computer's hard disk. All your other programs are available via the **Start** button at the bottom of the screen on the taskbar.

To open any application, either double-click the icon or click the Start button to open the Start menu. Click All Programs and another menu will open. Slowly move the pointer across to this menu and click your chosen application (see Figure 1.3).

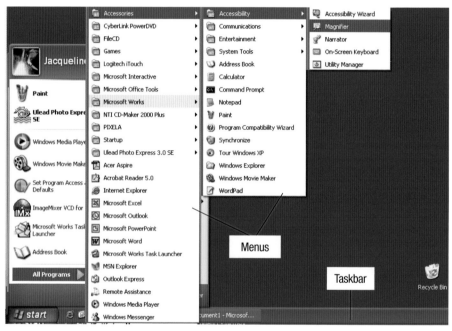

Figure 1.3

Other useful features of the Start menu include:

- a list of commonly used programs you have 'pinned' to the menu

- your main working storage areas (for example, My Documents)

- a Run option for starting up a CD or DVD

- search facilities to help find lost files or programs

- a Help menu (see Figure 1.4).

6

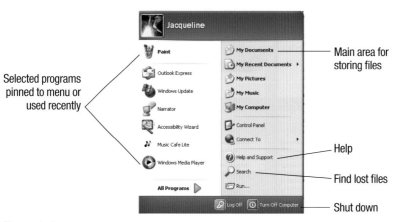

Selected programs
pinned to menu or
used recently

Main area for
storing files

Help

Find lost files

Shut down

Figure 1.4

Turning the machine on and off

As you work, various temporary files will be created within the computer
that will be sorted out automatically before your next session. To enable
this process to take place, it is important to follow a systematic shutdown
procedure every time you finish work, rather than simply switch off.

To shut down properly, click the **Start** button at the bottom left of the
screen to open the Start menu. Click **Turn Off Computer**, and then click
Turn Off in the small box that appears (Figure 1.5). You may be reminded
to save changes to any open files you have been working on. The
machine should then shut down automatically.

If you do just switch off, next time you turn on
the computer it will need to check the system
thoroughly before you can see the desktop, and
this can take quite a few frustrating minutes.

Figure 1.5

Although not as drastic as turning the power off
completely, you may need to restart the computer
at some stage. This is because, at times, it seems
to freeze up and either the mouse won't work or
programs no longer open or close properly.

A quick way to bring it back to life is to keep holding down both the Ctrl and
Alt keys (see page 24 for an introduction to the keyboard) with one hand as
you press the Delete key once, lightly with the other. Doing this should open
a window (Figure 1.6) offering an **End Task** button that, if you click it, will
take you back to the desktop where everything should work normally again.
You can also switch to another application if you prefer.

From the desktop, there is a shortcut to opening the Display properties box – right-click on an empty part of the desktop and select **Properties** from the menu that appears.

Working with windows

You will find that working with most of the programs available on a computer means opening up a window on the screen. More than one window can be open at a time and these can be resized or moved around.

Although each software package has its own particular menus and shortcut toolbar buttons, there is a fundamental similarity between them that helps when you move from one to another or learn to use new programs. If you are new to Windows XP, try to familiarise yourself with the basic window design (see Figure 1.10) as the various components will be mentioned many times throughout the book.

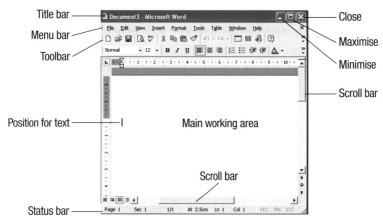

Figure 1.10

The parts of the window are:

Title bar:

This is blue when the window is **active** (ie when it is the current one in which you are working). The name of the program and file shows at the top left and the resizing buttons show top right:

Click this to minimise the window so that all you see is a labelled button on the taskbar. You can reopen the file or program at any time, to become the active window, by clicking the labelled button once. (If more than one file is open, clicking the button will display a list of files from which to select one to open.)

⊞ Restore Down (ie change) the window size so the desktop can be seen behind it. In this mode, the window can be moved or resized.

Move a window: Click in the title bar, keep holding down the mouse button and then drag the window across the screen.

Resize a window: Click and drag a border in or out when the pointer moved over the border changes from a single white arrow to a black two-way arrow ◄—►.

☐ Click to maximise the window to its largest size (this button alternates with the Restore Down button).

☒ Close the window – either a file or the program itself – by clicking this button.

Menu bar:

Basic menus – such as **File**, **Format**, **Edit**, **Tools** and **Help** – and those specific to the program you are using are all available here. In Windows XP you are also offered a task pane with shortcuts to common menu options. When you click the labelled menu button, a small range of options is made available (see Figure 1.11).

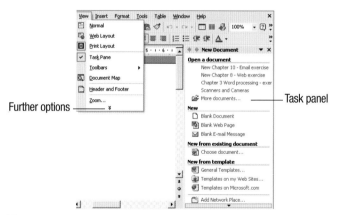

Further options

Task panel

Figure 1.11

If you click the double arrows at the end of the list, or rest your mouse on the open menu for a few seconds, you will see the full list of options. If an option appears grey, it means it is not available to you at that time (see Figure 1.12).

Not available

Figure 1.12

Toolbars:

These contain rows of buttons that act as shortcuts to the more common activities carried out when using your computer. Each toolbar has a set of buttons related to a particular group of tasks – for example, the **Drawing** toolbar offers you shortcuts to drawing lines or colouring shapes. Toolbar buttons display small pictures indicating the task they perform, but if you forget what they do, you can rest your mouse over the button and a definition will appear.

If you need extra toolbar buttons on screen, you can find them by clicking the down facing arrow at the end of the toolbar, and see the complete list of buttons available by selecting **Add or Remove Buttons**. You can add any complete toolbar from those available via the **View – Toolbars** menu, and add extra buttons permanently by selecting **Customize**, finding the button you want in the Commands window and dragging it up to your toolbar.

Scroll bars:

Click the arrows to move horizontally across or vertically up and down the page, or drag the grey box in the appropriate direction.

Status bar:

This provides information such as page numbers, cursor position, print or save status.

Taskbar:

This houses the Start menu that is always available and any open programs or files that have been minimised, shortcuts (eg to the desktop or internet), and useful information (eg date and time). Right-click the bar to select different ways to arrange several open windows on screen at the same time.

Getting organised

Once you start to use a computer, you'll soon find that you produce a large number of different files. Locating one again quickly can become quite difficult unless you store them systematically.

This chapter looks at how you can manage your computer files successfully. It focuses in particular on:

- filing on the desktop
- file management with Windows Explorer
- moving several files together
- creating new folders
- finding missing files
- creating a shortcut.

At the end of the chapter there are some suggested activities that will help you practise creating folders and moving files.

Filing on the desktop

Computer file management works on exactly the same principles as office or home filing. Instead of throwing all your correspondence into a single drawer, you probably have drop-files or special folders labelled 'insurance', 'car', 'tax', 'health', and so on, to hold certificates, letters and other relevant documents. In the same way, rather than saving every file directly into the single **My Documents** folder that is set aside as an area on the hard disk for saving work, you need to set up new, individually labelled folders within My Documents where all your work on specific topics can be stored safely. (Later in this book you will see that folders are also used to store favourite web page addresses [see Chapter 7] and organise your emails [see Chapter 9].)

From the **Start** menu, open **My Documents**. Inside will be any folders already created for you (yellow boxes) as well as any files you have saved so far. Each file will display an icon showing the application with which it was created.

Select
appropriate
option

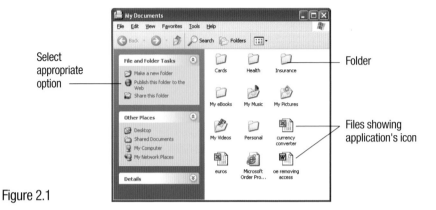

Folder

Files showing
application's icon

Figure 2.1

To create a new folder inside My Documents to hold files you produce relating to insurance matters for example, select the option in the task pane labelled **Make a New Folder** (see Figure 2.1). A new yellow folder will appear with the temporary name New Folder showing over a blue background in a naming box (Figure 2.2).

Anything you enter will automatically replace this blue selected text, so enter 'Insurance', for example, and then press Enter. (If you make a mistake, right-click the folder, select **Rename** by clicking this menu option with the left mouse button and try again.) You can make other folders, such as Health or Personal, in the same way.

Figure 2.2

Once you have created a folder in which to place all your insurance-related files, you can subdivide the folder even further by creating subfolders. These could then each contain files relating to one aspect of insurance, such as house details and car details. To do this, first open the 'parent' insurance folder before using the task pane option. The new subfolder that appears will be inside the parent folder (see Figure 2.3) and the folders structure on your computer will look like Figure 2.4.

Figure 2.3

14

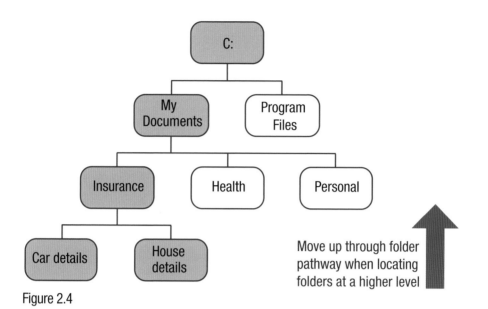

Figure 2.4

Once you have created some folders, you can move your files into them (or make copies to place there) very easily. Click on a file (eg Mini 2008 insurance) and select **Move this file**. When the window opens, select the destination folder from the list and click **Move**. To copy the file but leave the original in place, select the **Copy** option.

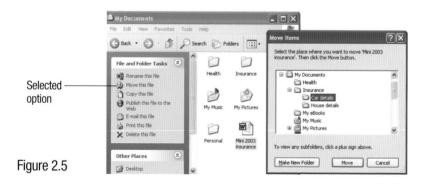

Selected option

Figure 2.5

An alternative method is to carry out the move in three stages:

1. Select the file and right-click to open a menu. Click **Cut** (to move it) or **Copy** (to copy it). It will be placed in part of the computer memory called the Clipboard.

Figure 2.6

15

2 Now look in subfolders or go up one or more levels until you can open the destination folder .

3 Right-click and select **Paste** and the file will appear inside the window of the open folder.

Deleting files or folders is simple – just select them and press the Delete key, remembering to move out any files you want to keep before deleting a folder.

Files that are deleted are actually moved to a different folder – the Recycle Bin – and are only removed permanently when this is emptied. Do this by opening the Recycle Bin on the desktop, and selecting **Empty the Recycle Bin**. Be careful, however, as this option is not available for files on floppy disks; files are permanently removed with immediate effect if you delete any stored here.

File management with Windows Explorer

An alternative way to manage files is to open the file management program, Windows Explorer, by clicking the **Folders** button inside My Documents (see Figure 2.7). Your window will now be divided into two panes – on the left the folders-only structure, and on the right the first level of contents of any selected folder, including any subfolders and files.

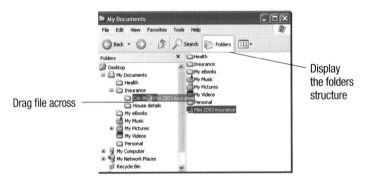

Figure 2.7

If you had saved some files onto a CD and wanted to create folders for them, open My Computer and select **CD Drive (D:)**; otherwise, click **My Documents**. You may need to click the + in a small box next to the drive to expand the folders/subfolders structure (to contract the structure, click the –).

To create a new folder, select the 'parent' disk or folder in the left pane and go to **File – New – Folder**.

You can now move or copy files into folders by selecting them and then dragging them across from the right to left panes. Once the destination folder turns blue, let go of the mouse to add your file.

If you click the right mouse button, you open a menu of options and can select either the **Copy** or **Move** option.

Copy Here
Move Here
Create Shortcuts Here

Cancel

Figure 2.8

Moving several files together

For a major reorganisation, you may have several files to move across. Instead of dragging them one at a time, you can select either a range of files or non-adjacent files so that, when you drag one, you will move them all together. (It may help if the files are arranged as a list rather than as large icons – if you want to change the arrangement go to **View – List**).

Selecting a range of files

1 Click the first in the range.

2 Hold down the Shift key – if you're not sure where this is look at the diagram on page 24.

3 Click the last in the range – all files between first and last will be selected.

4 Drag one across and they will move together.

Selecting non-adjacent files

1 Click to select the first file.

2 Hold down the Ctrl key.

3 Click other, individual files – all will remain selected.

Creating new folders as they are needed

Within any of the main applications, such as Word, Excel or PowerPoint, you may decide that a current piece of work should be placed in a folder that has not yet been created. Instead of opening Windows Explorer or returning to the desktop, you can create a folder at the same time as you save your work.

When you click the **Save** button, you will open the Save As box where you decide on the name and location for your file. Go up through the folder pathway if necessary to open the parent folder. If you now click the **Create New Folder** button , you will be able to create and name a new folder inside. Click OK so that it appears in the Save In box. Now when you name your work and click **Save**, the file will be saved directly into your new folder (see Figure 2.9).

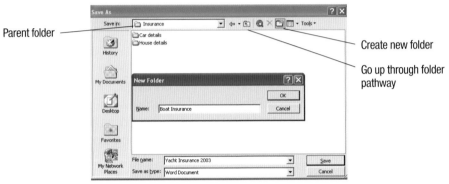

Parent folder

Create new folder

Go up through folder pathway

Figure 2.9

Finding missing files

However good your filing system, there will always be files, folders or programs that you cannot find. Fortunately, Windows XP has an excellent searching facility that you can use.

Files have different extensions at the end of their names (as well as displaying a different icon) depending on which application was used to create them. Here are some of the common file types:

.doc – Word document
.dot – Word template
.xls – Excel workbook
.ppt – PowerPoint
.html – web page
.txt – text file
.bmp – bitmap image file
.jpg – JPEG image file

To locate a file (or folder), select **Search** from the **Start** menu or click the **Search** button in the **My Documents** window (see Figure 2.10). You can choose what type of object you want to find. (You also have the option to connect to the internet and search for a relevant web page.)

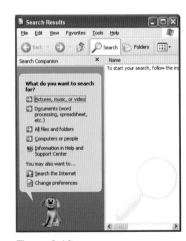

Figure 2.10

Having selected your choice, enter as much information as you can about the lost item, and then click **Search**. Scroll down or click **Advanced Options** to enter more specific criteria, such as how old it might be.

Any matching files or programs will be listed, and you can finish the search or try again.

If you select the option to find all files and folders, make sure that the Look In box contains the correct folder location (eg My Documents) or a new one (eg Holidays), which you can search for by clicking in the box or using the **Browse** button. If you have no clue where the file was stored, select the correct drive, for example, (C:) to look on your hard disk or (D:) drive if you are searching a CD.

Now enter the full folder or filename and any extension – for example, Adobe (folder name) or invitation to openday.doc (file name). If you only know part of the name, use * for the missing characters – for example, invitation*.doc or *openday.doc or *open*.* (If you only know some of the words in the name, you can enter these in the Word or phrase box instead, but this is a much slower search.)

To find all files of a particular file type, enter *. (extension) – for example, *.bmp to find all Bitmap picture files.

Figure 2.11

Figure 2.12

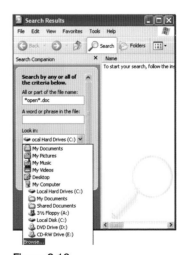

Figure 2.13

19

Creating a shortcut

If you regularly want to refer to a particular file, or run a program that is buried deep amongst your computer files, you can create a shortcut to it on the desktop.

One method of creating a shortcut is to find the file from My Computer or inside My Documents and right-click to give you the option to **Send to – Desktop** (see Figure 2.14).

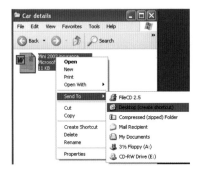

Figure 2.14

Shortcuts created on the desktop normally show a small arrow, and you can change the name if you want to by clicking the name box once, or by right-clicking and selecting **Rename**.

Figure 2.15

You can also start on an empty part of the desktop, right-click and select **New – Shortcut**. Browse through your program files until you find your target and click **Open** to place the filename in the box (program files usually have the extension .exe), **Next** for your own choice of name, and then OK to create the shortcut (Figure 2.16).

Figure 2.16

20

Organise your work activities

Practise:

- creating folders
- moving files into folders.

1. In My Documents or any chosen folder location, create a new folder and give it a suitable name e.g. Computer Practice.

2. Now create some subfolders inside it – for example, Word Processing, Spreadsheets, Web Addresses.

3. If you have any files on your computer – practise moving or copying them into one of your new folders.

4. Now move them out again to their original destination.

5. Finally, make a few folders and subfolders that will be useful later. You may also like to delete your practice folders.

Getting the most from Word

Even if you are a slow typist, word processing has many advantages:

- Documents are far easier to read than handwritten material.
- Copies of all your work are simple to save on disk.
- Making changes no longer requires typing everything again.
- It looks far more professional for business or official documents.
- There is a wide range of special effects you can incorporate into your work.
- If you use email, you can attach word-processed documents to your messages and send them at the same time.

There are numerous books devoted to Microsoft Word as well as the other main software applications, and you may want to look at one of these for a detailed introduction to word processing. This chapter outlines the basic steps you can take to get started, as well as showing you some of the possibilities offered by the program. There is also a labelled keyboard picture on page 24. The chapter ends with suggested activities to provide practice in the basic skills covered.

The chapter looks in detail at:

- creating and changing a document
- saving your document
- improving the appearance of your document
- moving or copying text
- getting help
- previewing and printing
- letters
- AutoText
- templates
- dates
- working with pictures
- labels and envelopes.

Creating and changing a document

You open Microsoft Word either by clicking the icon on your desktop or **Start** menu **W**, or by selecting the program from your program listings after clicking **Start – All Programs**. When you have opened Word, you are presented with a blank screen – 'a clean sheet of paper' – and can start typing straightaway. (On one side you will also be offered a task pane with shortcuts to various facilities, but you can close this by clicking the black cross in the top right-hand corner if you want to see more of the screen.) The text will appear at the position marked by the cursor, a flashing black vertical bar, which will be a short way in from the top left-hand corner of the screen to leave space for the top and left margins. (See Figure 1.10 on page 10 in Chapter 1.)

Using the same techniques as typing on a typewriter (eg holding down the Shift key to produce a capital letter or symbol at the top of a key, or pressing the space bar between words), you will be able to start creating your first document. You will notice that the computer **wraps** the text down the page for you, so that you don't need to take any action to start typing on a new line when you reach the right-hand margin of the page.

For a title in capital letters, first press the Caps Lock key, and then press it again when you want to use both upper and lower case (see Figure 3.1).

Editing

To correct mistakes or add extra text, you will need to move the cursor to a different position. Click the mouse pointer in position on screen when it shows a thin vertical bar or press the arrow key on your keyboard that points in the appropriate direction. Pressing the Home key moves the cursor to the start of a line, and the End key will move it to the end of a line. Hold the Ctrl key as you press either the Home or the End key to move to the start or end of the whole document.

Once you have a page of text, you can use the scroll bars to move up or down – either click the arrow at the top or bottom of the bar or drag the grey square box in the appropriate direction. The keys labelled Page Up or Page Down will also allow you to move through large blocks of text.

Delete incorrect letters next to the cursor with the Backspace key (erasing to the left) or Delete key (erasing to the right). When you type your new letters they will be inserted in the space. If you make a mistake, such as deleting the wrong text, you can click the **Undo** button ↰ to step back through your actions.

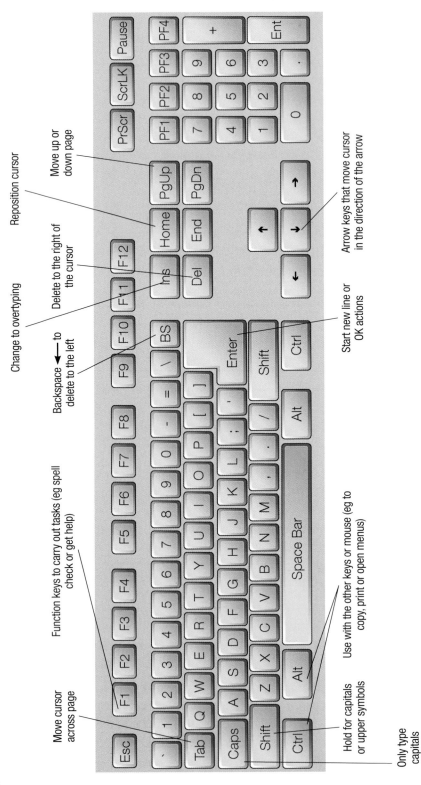

Move cursor across page

Function keys to carry out tasks (eg spell check or get help)

Change to overtyping

Reposition cursor

Backspace ← to delete to the left

Delete to the right of the cursor

Move up or down page

Arrow keys that move cursor in the direction of the arrow

Start new line or OK actions

Hold for capitals or upper symbols

Use with the other keys or mouse (eg to copy, print or open menus)

Only type capitals

Figure 3.1

Occasionally, extra text replaces the original rather than allowing you to insert it. This means you have pressed the Insert key by mistake and have changed to overtyping. To return to normal, press this key again.

To start a new paragraph, you need to press the Enter key (sometimes called the Return key) to move the cursor to the beginning of a new line, and you can keep pressing it if you want a larger gap before typing again. As it takes any text to its right down the page with it, you will need to ensure first of all that the cursor is at the end of your text. Otherwise you can easily split words or sentences. (If you do this by mistake, pressing the Backspace key will join your words up again by deleting the space you made.)

Spelling

Checking your spelling or grammar is very easy with Word, as the computer will underline any 'suspect' words with red or green wavy lines. To correct one word, right-click the line with the mouse and select an alternative if it is presented.

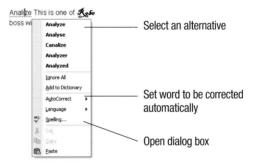

Figure 3.2

To check the whole document, click the **Spelling and Grammar** button 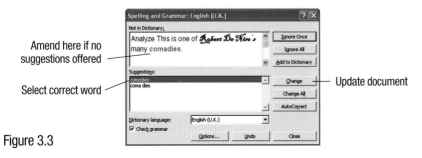. This will open a dialog box in which you can change words manually or select from choices available in the suggestions pane. To update your document, click **Change**, otherwise click an **Ignore** option and continue checking. You can end the check at any time by clicking **Close**.

Figure 3.3

Saving your document

So that you won't lose your work because of a mistake or any technical problems, it is always a good idea to save your new document early, and then update it regularly as you make further changes.

On clicking the **Save** toolbar button 🖫 you will open a Save As dialog box. You need to specify where you want to save your work (eg into the My Documents folder or onto a CD) and what recognisable name to give it (see Figure 3.4). Once you have checked or amended the information in the Save In and File name boxes, press the Enter key or click the Save button and your work will be saved. You will see that the Title bar across the top of your screen will now display the file's new name rather than the temporary title Document 1. Once saved and named, clicking the Save button will update the document automatically.

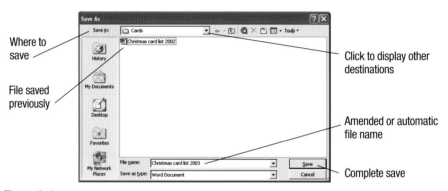

Figure 3.4

Occasionally you might want to keep several versions of the same document. In this case, you need to select **Save As** from the **File** menu and rename or choose a different location for the file before clicking **Save**.

Once files have been saved and closed, they can be opened again at any time. Click the **Open** button on the toolbar 🖆 and then browse through your folders until the correct one is open in the Look In box. Click the file to select it and click **Open** or press Enter (see Figure 3.5).

When you close a file but not Word, you will see a grey background and limited toolbar. Click the **New** button 🗋 to start a new document.

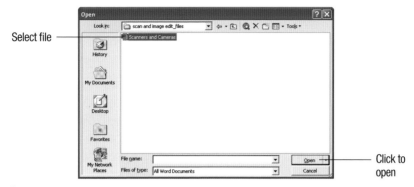

Select file

Click to open

Figure 3.5

Changing the look of your document

The appearance of your document (its **format**) depends on the formatting settings pre-defined within Word that are known as the **default** settings. To underline a heading, or increase the size of your text, for example, you will need to change the settings. This can be carried out before you start typing, or you can select particular words or sections of text and then apply new formatting just to this selection.

There are various ways to select letters, words or blocks of text, using either mouse or keyboard. Selected text will always appear as white letters on a black background (you may have noticed this happening by mistake as you created your document) and you can take off the selection by clicking the mouse button anywhere on the screen away from the left margin.

Review of New Film

Analyze this is one of Robert De Niro's many comedies. boss with

Figure 3.6

27

- To select one word, double-click it with the mouse.

- To select several words or a block of text, click at one end and then hold down the mouse button as you drag the mouse across the entry.

- If you prefer to use the keyboard, click at the start and then hold down the Shift key as you press an arrow key in the relevant direction. For text that extends below the screen, click to place the cursor at the start of a section, use the scroll bar to move to the end of the section and hold the Shift key as you click the mouse again.

- For a complete line of text, click the mouse when the pointer in the left margin shows a right-facing arrow. Click and drag to select several lines.

- To select the entire document, hold Ctrl and press the letter A. Alternatively, open the **Edit** menu and click **Select All**.

Once you have selected some words, you can use the toolbar buttons to change them to **bold**, *italic* or <u>underlined</u> **B** *I* <u>U</u>. The selected toolbar button will show as a blue box. To revert to the default settings, you may need to click the toolbar buttons off again before continuing your typing. You can also apply a colour or alter the size or type of character (font) from the drop-down lists available. Many boxes on screen have a small downward-facing arrow next to them – click the arrow to display a list of possible choices you can make.

Figure 3.7

Alternatively, you can click the toolbar button 🄰 to open the **Styles and Formatting** task pane for a combined set of font formats (see Figure 3.8), or go to **File – Format** and click **Font** to open the dialog box. Select from the drop-down lists or checkboxes and preview the changes to your selected text before accepting them by clicking OK (see Figure 3.9).

Click button to
open Task Panel

Font colour

Figure 3.8

Figure 3.9

Paragraphs can also be changed so that, for example, text is centred on the page or positioned on the right (see Figure 3.10), or long documents are justified where text is spread evenly across the page. You can also change line spacing to double or 1.5, and move the start of a paragraph in from the margin using the **Indent** option (see Figure 3.11). If choices aren't available as toolbar buttons, open the **Format – Paragraph** dialog box to select and preview alternatives. (If carrying on typing, don't forget to press the Enter key and change the settings if you want to revert back to an earlier alignment or spacing option.)

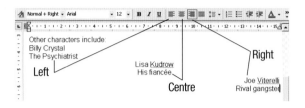

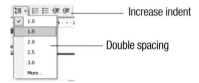

Other characters include:
Billy Crystal
The Psychiatrist

Left

Lisa Kudrow
His fiancée

Right

Joe Viterelli
Rival gangster

Centre

Figure 3.10

Increase indent

Double spacing

Figure 3.11

In this way you can make a variety of changes to the appearance of your documents with just a couple of clicks of the mouse.

Moving or copying text

Once you have typed a large block of text, you may decide to position it elsewhere or copy it to another part of the document. Rather than type it all again, you can save time by moving or copying it – either select it and then click and drag it to a new position with the mouse or follow these four simple steps known as Cut/Copy & Paste:

1 Select the text you want to move or copy.

2 Click the **Cut** button ✂ (available when you right-click the text, from the **Edit** menu or on the toolbar) to move text, or **Copy** button 📋 to leave the original in place.

3 Click in the new position for the text so the cursor is flashing on screen.

4 Click the **Paste** button 📋. The text will now appear, and you will be offered a choice of reformatting or leaving it in the original state.

The technique relies on text being stored temporarily in part of the computer memory known as the Office Clipboard. This can store up to 24 objects (such as text or pictures) so that you can copy many items and paste them into documents together or selectively. If not visible, you can open the Clipboard from the **Edit** menu.

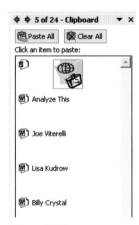

Figure 3.12

Getting help

Within each program, there are usually two or three different ways to get help. One way is to type a question or short phrase into the on-screen Ask a Question box and press Enter to see a list of links to relevant answers that you can then click to view.

A wider choice is offered if you open the **Help** menu and select **Microsoft Word Help**. Here you can choose to see an overview of different topics (Content), ask a question (Answer Wizard), search an index using keywords or connect to the internet for further help (see Figure 3.14). The menu also offers you the option to activate the office assistant, providing on-screen shortcuts to various activities, or to display a definition of anything you click if you first select **What's This?**

Figure 3.13

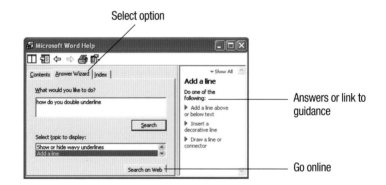

Figure 3.14

Previewing and printing

When you are happy with your document – and as long as a suitable printer has been installed correctly, is turned on and has paper in it – you can print a single copy by clicking the **Print** toolbar button 🖨. Before that, it is always a good idea to preview the work by clicking the **Print Preview** button 🔍. Now you can see if you need to close up any gaps or change margins or page orientation (see Figure 3.15). One useful button is labelled **Shrink to Fit**. If just a few words of your text have gone over to a second page, this will reduce the font slightly so that you can force the text to fit on one page.

Turn off magnifier to work in this view

Choose how many pages to view

Return to your document

Shrink to fit

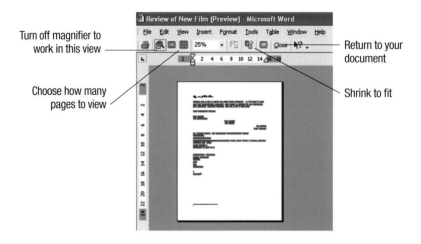

Figure 3.15

Amend the margins by moving your mouse pointer over the area between the grey and white sections of the ruler. Hold down the button when you see a two-way arrow and drag the dotted line representing the margin to a new position (see Figure 3.16).

You can also open the File menu and select Page Setup to set margins exactly, set the printer to print on different sized paper, or change from portrait to landscape orientation (where the long sides of the paper are across the top and bottom) (see Figure 3.17).

Drag margin boundary

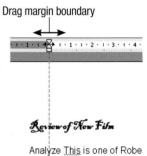

Figure 3.16

Set paper size

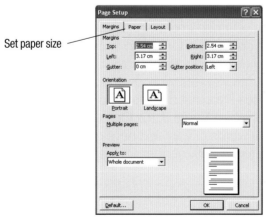

Figure 3.17

For a range of options, such as printing several copies, or selecting particular pages to print, you will need to choose options in the **Print** dialog box opened via the **File** menu.

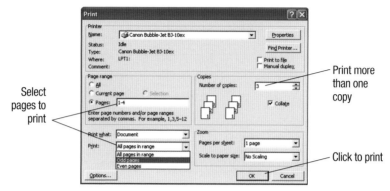

Select pages to print

Print more than one copy

Click to print

Figure 3.18

Letters

Writing official letters can be a chore. Fortunately, there are a number of useful features in Word to make the job easier. If you play a role in a local society, association or charity, for example, these shortcuts can help you save a great deal of time and effort when carrying out your administrative tasks. You can:

- use shortcuts to enter commonly used words or dates automatically in documents
- create templates to use over and over again
- make text look more attractive by inserting pictures from a ready-made gallery, a disk or the web
- produce address labels to save time when writing to a large number of people.

Layout

Word-processed letters follow the same rules as those applied when writing by hand. People often save time by leaving out the commas after each line of an address and by starting each line of text at the left margin (ie left aligned).

A typical letter that might be sent out by the secretary of a local association enclosing the annual programme of events is shown in Figure 3.19.

Hambledean Allotment Association
Greys Road
Stoke
ST5 7RG

Mr P White
25 Abbey Way
Stoke
ST5 2LR

25 November 2008

Dear Peter

Please find enclosed a copy of this year's calendar of events. I think you'll agree
that the committee has put together a very interesting programme.

Do look through and let me know which talks you would like to attend, so that I
can arrange suitable refreshments.

I look forward to seeing you at the summer garden party.

Yours sincerely

Mavis Applewood
Secretary

Figure 3.19

Creating new pages

Sometimes you may want to start a second page at an exact point,
rather than let this happen when you reach the bottom of the first page.
This can be done by creating a page break (sometimes known as a hard
break). Position the cursor in front of the word you want to start on a
new page and, holding Ctrl down with one hand, press the Enter key (or
select **Break – Page Break** from the **Insert** menu).

You will see the following on the page:

..............Page Break..............

If you want to remove the break, do this by clicking on the dotted line
and pressing the Delete key.

AutoText

One way to save time is to store common text such as an address (which
could even include a picture as part of a logo) as AutoText. This can then
be inserted automatically into any document with a few keystrokes.

Set out the address as you want it to appear in your documents and then select the entire block of text. Open the **Insert** menu, select the **AutoText – New** option and in the **Name** box type in a few letters or a short word to identify the selection – eg 'home' or 'haa' (short for Hambledean Allotment Association). Then click **OK**.

Figure 3.20

Next time you want to insert the address into your letter, type 'haa' and then press the function key F3 that you will find at the top of your keyboard. The address will appear.

Templates

To reproduce a complete layout that could include your address and some text in your chosen font, together with your letter ending, you may prefer to create a template that you can use every time you type a similar letter. The template is kept with others in a Templates folder and remains unchanged when you use it to create your documents. (See Chapter 2 for more information on folders.)

Open Word, or start a new, blank document, and type as much of your letter as you want to save and use repeatedly. Then click the **Save** button to open the **Save As** window.

To save a template rather than a normal Word document, select **Document Template** from the drop-down list in the **Save As Type** box (see Figure 3.21). Once you do this, you will see that the **Save In** box shows the Templates folder. Name the file (eg HAA-letter) and click **Save**.

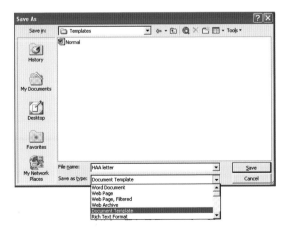

Figure 3.21

To use the template in future, go to **File – New** and in the task pane click **General Templates**. Select the template from those showing in the window and, with the **Create New Document** option chosen, click OK (see Figure 3.22). Your basic letter layout will appear and you can now continue to write and save your letter in the normal way.

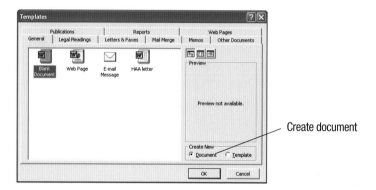

Figure 3.22

You can use the same method to create templates for a range of documents that you produce regularly, such as headed notepaper, invitations, programmes, newsletters, reports or minutes of meetings.

To save even more time, go to **File – New – General Templates** first of all and check the Template tabs (eg Letters and Faxes, Publications, Memos) to see if the proposed document already exists as a template. Then, if you want to create your own customised version, you can select the option **Create New Template** before you open the example. After making changes to suit your own needs, save the amended template (temporarily titled Template1) with a different name. Note that in some cases, you may have to reinsert your Microsoft Office CD to find the selected template.

Dates

Word can put in today's date for you with a few mouse clicks. Position the cursor where you want the date to appear and select **Insert – Date and Time** to open the dialog box. Select your preferred style of date and then click OK to return to your document (see Figure 3.23). If you will be delaying printing but want that day's date in your document, click the **Update** box.

To save time in future, click the **Default** button when you first select a style of date so that your preferred format is always selected every time you open the Date and Time dialog box.

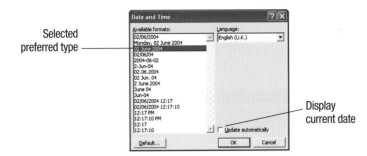

Selected
preferred type

Display
current date

Figure 3.23

Working with pictures

To enhance the appearance of your stationery or any document you produce, you may like to include a picture. If used often, it can be saved with a template or inserted each time you write a letter by adding it to your AutoText list.

You can choose to use pictures available in the ready-made Clip Art Gallery installed with Word, from a CD-ROM, the web or from file (ie insert an image that has previously been saved on disk). Once it appears on the page, you can resize or reposition it or carry out more detailed editing using the **Picture** toolbar.

Inserting Clip Art

To open up the gallery, click the **Insert Clip Art** toolbar button 🖼 on the **Drawing** toolbar, or go to **Insert – Picture – Clip Art**. (To display the toolbar, either click the **Drawing** button 🖋 or go to **View – Toolbars – Drawing**.)

An **Insert Clip Art** task pane will appear and you can type in a keyword in the search text box and click the **Search** button, or open the list of Selected collections and restrict the categories from which to search (see Figure 3.24).

Type in
keywords

Choose a
category

Figure 3.24

37

When the pictures appear, scroll down until you find one that you like. Click it once and it will appear in your document, although you may need to insert the Microsoft Office CD first. You can always repeat the search by clicking **Modify**.

Figure 3.25

Select the picture in your document by clicking it to show a black border with small squares (sizing handles) round the edges. In this state you can amend it in one of the following three ways:

- If you change your mind and don't like it after all, just press the Delete key. You can now return to the gallery and find another picture.

- To change its size, move the mouse pointer over any sizing handle and, when it shows a two-way arrow, gently click and drag the border in or out (see Figure 3.26).

- Finally, use the normal Word alignment buttons to centre the picture or realign it to the left or right of the page.

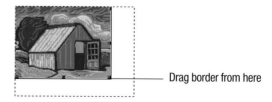

Figure 3.26

Moving pictures around

You may want to have more control over the position of a picture than is allowed by the alignment settings, and to do this you can insert it into a **text box**. This box, with the picture inside, can then be dragged round the screen to any position. (You can also use text boxes for captions, labels or any extra text on the page.)

Click the **Text Box** button ▣ on the **Drawing** toolbar, and then, to create a box of the right size, either click on screen or click and drag when the mouse pointer shows a small cross. A flashing cursor will appear inside the box where you would normally start typing your text.

Now, if you insert a Clip Art picture as normal it will appear inside the text box. You can also select a picture that has already been inserted and then click the **Text Box** button to situate it in the box, but you may then need to resize the picture to centre it correctly.

Move the mouse pointer over the selected text box edge, and when it shows a four-way arrow, you will be able to click and drag it across the screen. You can also resize either text box or picture by dragging one of the borders with the two-way arrow over a sizing handle.

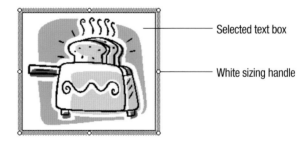

Figure 3.27

To remove the visible text box border, select it to show its thick edge and white sizing handles (see Figure 3.27) and then select **No Line** from the Line Colour palette on the **Drawing** toolbar (see Figure 3.28). Alternatively, emphasise the border using the line options available.

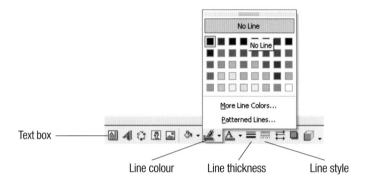

Text box

Line colour   Line thickness   Line style

Figure 3.28

Another way of dragging a picture is to change it into an object by selecting it and then clicking **Draw – Text Wrapping** on the **Drawing** toolbar. This option is normally used to set the way that text will wrap round a picture inserted in a document. After choosing a style such as Tight, you will find that the black sizing handles now appear as white circles and you can drag the picture round the screen. You can also rotate it by dragging the green circle at the end of the rotating arm (see Figure 3.29).

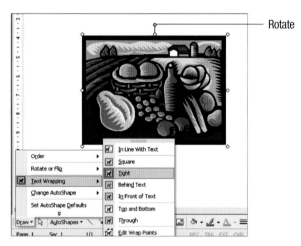

Rotate

Figure 3.29

Editing a picture

For more detailed changes, you need to right-click the picture and select **Show Picture Toolbar** (see Figure 3.30). You can open the Format dialog box to work with lines and background colours, or ungroup or edit the picture to change particular sections.

From the **Picture** toolbar, choose one of the following:

- **Image control**: create a black and white or greyscale image or fade it into the background as a watermark.

- **Contrast or Brightness**: click these up or down.

- **Compress**: reduce the size of the image – for example, to send with an email.

- **Crop**: cut off a section of the picture by clicking the button. You may see black bars appear round the picture. Move the pointer over one of these or a sizing handle and gently drag in the picture border when the mouse pointer shows the cropping symbol. When you let go, any part of the picture now left outside the border will disappear.

- **Text wrap**: choose how the text on the page will wrap round your picture.

- **Reset**: click if you have made too many changes and want to start again.

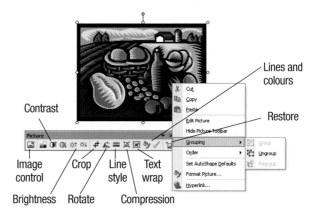

Figure 3.30

Pictures from elsewhere

Having a scanner or digital camera allows you to create and save a range of photos or drawings that can then be inserted into your word-processed documents. Alternatively, you can borrow or buy a CD-ROM full of images you can use.

To insert an image into an open document, minimise the document (see page 10) and then select and open the picture. Click the **Copy** toolbar button, restore your Word document from the taskbar, click in place with

41

the cursor and then click **Paste**. (You can also insert a picture by locating it after opening the **Insert** menu, selecting **Picture – From File** and clicking the **Insert** button or pressing Enter.)

If you find a picture on the web that you'd like to store for future use (as long as it won't infringe any copyright), it is a very simple process to save this onto your computer. Right-click the mouse on the image and, from the short menu that appears, select **Save Picture As**. This will then open the normal Save As window and you can name and save the picture into an appropriate folder. As an alternative, select the **Copy** option and then you will be able to paste the picture straight from the web into your document (Figure 3.31).

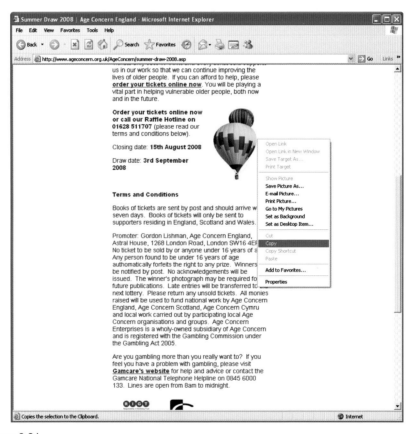

Figure 3.31

Labels and envelopes

If you are writing to a number of people, or want to prepare dinner party place names, put your return address on parcels or label storage boxes or jars of home-made jam, you can use the computer to print envelopes or produce labels.

For labels, open the **Tools** menu and select **Letters and Mailings – Envelopes and Labels**.

Figure 3.32

Click the appropriate tab (eg Labels) and select **Options** to choose the correct size of label sheets on which to print. Sheets with labels of different sizes are available from most stationers but, if necessary, click **New Label** to set your own size.

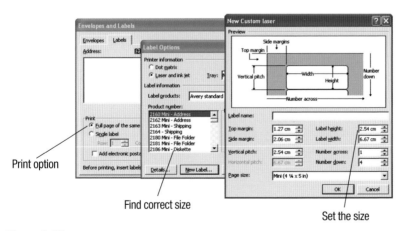

Print option

Find correct size

Set the size

Figure 3.33

To produce different labels on the same sheet, click **New Document** and type your text into the various label outlines. If the outlines are not visible, go to **Table – Show Gridlines**.

You can produce a sheet of identical labels by entering the text once into the Address window (see Figure 3.34).

43

Create an
envelope

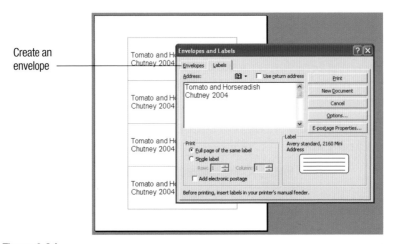

Figure 3.34

Click **Print** to print the labels straightaway or view them by clicking **New Document** and save them to print another time. Make sure that the setting is correct for a page of labels or a single label on one page.

Envelopes can be very simple to print. If you type your letter and select the recipient's address, going to **Tools** – **Letters and Mailings** – **Envelopes and Labels** will place your text in the Envelope window automatically. Otherwise, type it in directly, insert the envelope in the printer in the correct position and click **Print**.

Word-processing activities

Practise:

- amending text
- formatting text
- inserting a picture from file
- formatting pictures
- saving a new version of a file
- printing.

1. Open a new document and type some text.

2. Change several words.

3. Centre the heading and then:

   a. Increase the title font size and change the format, for example, make it bold or underlined.

   b. Reduce the text size of the rest of the document.

   c. Apply a different font (eg Arial, Times New Roman or Courier).

4. Add any relevant picture from file or the Clip Art Gallery.

5. Reduce it to roughly half its original size.

6. Change the image from colour to greyscale.

7. Save the final version of the document as Final Version and print one copy.

CHAPTER 4

Getting even more from Word

To produce leafets, flyers, newspaper advertisements, newsletters or other specialist stationery items, you don't need specialist software, as you can use many of the design tools available with your word-processing package. For example, you can display text in columns, add numbers or bullets to list items, border or shade sections of text, and insert special features, such as WordArt.

This chapter looks at how to do this in Word. It looks specifically at:

- creating a leaflet (including columns, lists, and borders and shading)
- using WordArt
- drawings
- tables.

Creating a leaflet

When you are designing a leaflet, you need to think about exactly where the text or pictures should be placed. For every A4 piece of paper, you may have sections that are blank or parts that will be created as a new document but printed on the reverse of the original, so you must take care when replacing the paper in the printer. You can also customise the page set-up by selecting **Paper size** and choosing differently sized paper on which to print.

Black and white can look very smart, especially if printed onto coloured paper. However, using a colour printer or taking your file on disk into a print shop may be worthwhile if you want the best colour effect or a large number of items produced.

One example of the type of leaflet you could produce is the Hambledean Allotment Association programme (see Figure 4.1), which is a three-fold leaflet based on two A4 documents printed on both sides of a single sheet of paper.

Figure 4.1

For this kind of leaflet, each page needs to be reorientated from upright (portrait) to lengthways (landscape) via the **File – Page Setup – Paper size** menu option, and then divided into three equal columns (see Figure 4.2). (A less ambitious leaflet could be produced based on two columns with a central fold.)

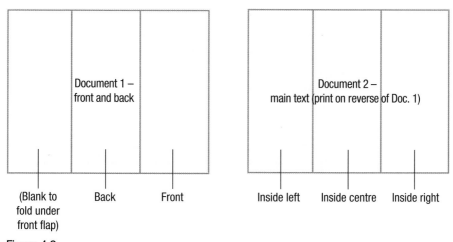

Figure 4.2

Columns of text

You can change to columns after entering text if you first select the block of text and then apply the change to the selected section, or you can set up column formatting first of all.

You can also insert pictures or drawings into the columns and decide where each column will break on the page.

For straightforward columns, simply click the **Column** toolbar button and drag the mouse across to set the number.

To choose which piece of text begins in column 2 or 3, rather than leaving it to wrap round at the bottom of the page, click in front of the first word and select **Insert – Break – Column Break**.

For more options, you need to open the Columns dialog box by selecting **Format – Columns** (see Figure 4.3). Here you can amend the column widths by selecting identical or uneven columns, and, if necessary, altering the exact measurements displayed in the Width and spacing section. You can also add a dividing line and apply the formatting to particular sections of a document. This is important if you want to leave a central heading or earlier text unaltered, as you can select **Apply to: This point forward**, or **Selected text**.

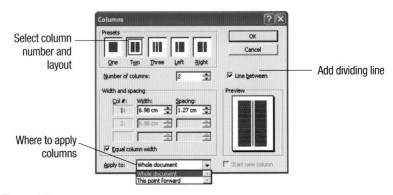

Figure 4.3

When you want to return to a normal layout after creating columns, press Enter to move to a new line, open the Columns dialog box again and select one column: **Apply to: This point forward**.

For Document 1 (ie the front/back of the Hambledean leaflet), you would need to format three columns and then insert a column break straightaway, leaving a blank first column that will fold inside the front page. This moves the cursor to the beginning of column 2, where you need to press the Enter key several times to move down the page. Now you can type in the contact details. These should be aligned centrally and will be visible at the back of the programme. You will then need to create the front of the leaflet in column 3.

Using WordArt

To make your text stand out, instead of simply selecting an unusual font and size, you can insert a text object created in a separate package – Microsoft WordArt. This can be shaped, coloured or stretched and will replace a heading or other normal text.

This is Times New Roman size 14 text

This is Times New Roman WordArt

To do this for the main title, click the **WordArt** button on the **Drawing** toolbar. From the gallery of styles that appears, select your preferred example (although this can be changed later) and click OK (see Figure 4.4).

You are taken to the Edit WordArt Text window (see Figure 4.5) and can now type in your text.

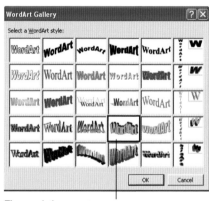

Figure 4.4   Select example

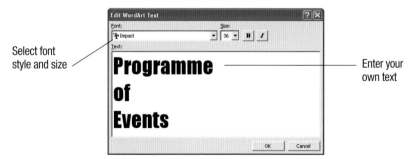

Select font
style and size

Enter your
own text

Figure 4.5

Make changes to font type and style using the toolbar at the top of the window and then click OK to return to your document.

Use the **WordArt** toolbar that appears to make various changes, such as apply a different colour, reorientate the text or increase spaces between letters (see Figure 4.6). To go back to the WordArt editing box to alter the text, click the **Edit Text** toolbar button or double-click the WordArt object. To return to the document, click OK.

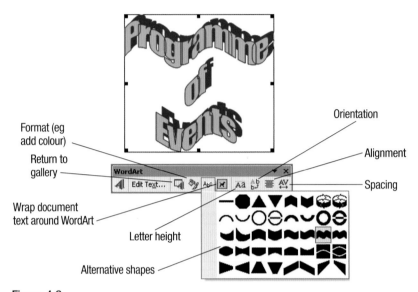

Orientation

Format (eg add colour)

Return to gallery

Alignment

Spacing

Wrap document text around WordArt

Letter height

Alternative shapes

Figure 4.6

If you want to drag the WordArt to a new position, apply a text wrap option from the **Drawing** toolbar, as you did with pictures (see page 40).

For other text on the front of the leaflet, either type word-processed text as normal or, for more control over its position, click and draw text boxes and enter basic details such as dates, names or other information into these. Move the boxes into different positions and format the text with appropriate types and sizes of letters.

Drawings

You don't have to be a great artist to produce quite attractive effects using the **Drawing** toolbar options (see Figure 4.7). There are ready-made shapes (AutoShapes) – such as lines, rectangles, circles, arrows or stars – that are inserted in the same way that you insert Text Boxes; that is, click on the button and then click on screen or click and drag the shape when the pointer shows a small cross. You can also use the freestyle 'pencil', but may need to double-click the mouse to release the pointer. Once your shape is on screen, you can add a border, fill it with colour, change its shape, flip or rotate it to point in a different direction.

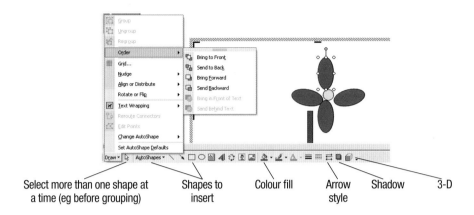

Select more than one shape at   Shapes to   Colour fill   Arrow   Shadow   3-D
a time (eg before grouping)   insert   style

Figure 4.7

In Windows XP, drawings will appear within a box called the drawing canvas. This allows you to move several objects together on the page. If you don't like using it, you can remove it by going to **Tools – Options – General** and removing the tick next to the box labelled: Automatically create drawing canvas when inserting AutoShapes.

You can layer drawing objects on top of one another, and use the **Order** option to send one shape behind another or behind text already present on screen. (This is very important if you want to emphasise text within a coloured box and still read the words.)

As with pictures (see pages 37–42), selected objects show sizing handles and you must see these before any toolbar options take effect. Dragging a white sizing handle, for example, will change the shape; dragging the green circle will change the direction.

If you create a complex drawing with several shapes and want to treat it as one object, perhaps to resize or move it to another part of the document, draw a box round it with the Select Objects arrow pointer and then select **Draw – Group**. To edit one part, select **Ungroup** and, finally, **Regroup**.

As well as creating drawings yourself using the Word drawing tools, you can use a separate package such as Microsoft Paint, which is available from the **Start – All Programs – Accessories** menu. You can also insert images from Clip Art (see page 37), a CD-ROM, or the world wide web, or images that have been scanned in or produced using a digital camera if you have the equipment. Note that the colour or sharpness of different images will vary, depending on the software used to create them. Common image file types you may come across include TIFF (.tif), bitmap (.bmp) or GIF (.gif) (file extensions are explained in Chapter 2 on page 18).

With the back and front sections complete, you are now ready to create Document 2, the (inside) main programme text.

Either type the text as a normal document and then select it and apply three columns to your selection, or set the column formatting first and type the first set of details in column 1 (see Figure 4.8).

- **22 September:** Preparing the Ground. Talk and demonstration of garden tools by staff at the Howbye Garden Centre.
- **18 October:** Quiz Night in the Hambledean Hall.
- **24 November:** Bulbs for Spring. Talk by Harry Spendle.
- **20 December:** Christmas Ball. Music by the *Skinflints*. Prizes presented by the Lord Mayor.

- **18 February:** Getting the Most from your Catalogues. Talk by Martin Potter.
- **27 March:** Visit to the Hawthorne Castle Gardens. Book early to avoid disappointment.
- **24 April:** Hanging Baskets. Demonstration by Serena Hamilton of Global Flowers.
- **17 May:** Fertilisers, Sprays or Organic? Discussion chaired by Fred Peters.

- **29 June:** Trip to the Lake District Conservancy Centre.
- **17 July:** Dahlias. Talk by Gladys Whittle. Bring along diseased plants for her expert advice.
- **15 August:** Garden Party and Root Vegetables competition.
- In the evening, hosting BBC Gardeners' Question Time in the Hambledean Hall. Book early!

Figure 4.8

You will need to insert a column break at the correct point, for example, before the February talk, so that the details start at the top of column 2, and again in front of the June trip. You may also need to edit the text or column width, to make sure the columns look roughly equal.

Lists

Bullets or numbers help break up dense text and make it easier to read. You will see that the events in the programme are displayed as a bulleted list.

There are two different ways to produce lists:

1 If you type the list without formatting, but place each item on a new line, you can then select all the text and click on the **Numbering** or **Bullets** toolbar buttons.

2 You can click on screen and then click the appropriate toolbar button before typing the first item. The first number or bullet will appear automatically and every time you press Enter a new one will be displayed.

Choose from a range of number or bullet styles by opening the **Format – Bullets and Numbering** dialog box (see Figure 4.9).

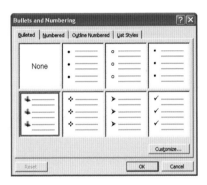

Figure 4.9

You can change the spacing between text and bullets/numbers via the **Customize** button, and then click **Bullet** to view the gallery of further styles.

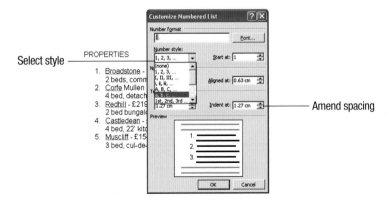

Figure 4.10

Whenever you want a line without a number or bullet, place the cursor in the line and click off the toolbar button, clicking the **Increase Indent** button ![icon] if the text is out of line. You can also create the same effect by holding the Shift key as you press Enter while you are typing the list.

Borders and shading

You may like to make the text stand out with a border and/or shading. Many different effects are possible using the **Format – Borders and Shading** menu options (see Figure 4.11).

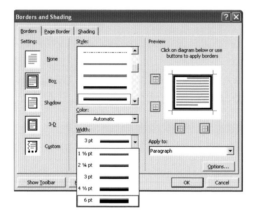

Figure 4.11

You can select a paragraph or section and add a surrounding border and/or shade the background (and there are even various lines and styles, including small pictures, which can be used to border a complete page).

To border just the text, select it first and then apply the effects to text and not paragraph. If you want the border to extend a small way past the text, but not across the complete page, border the paragraph, then select **Format – Paragraph** and indent the border both left and right by increasing the measurements in the Indents and Spacing dialog box.

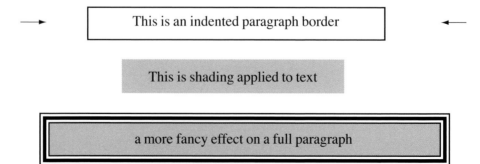

To continue typing below bordered text, double-click the mouse pointer to place the cursor on the page. (In earlier versions of Word, it was hard to 'get out' of a bordered paragraph. A good tip is to press Enter a few times to clear yourself a space before going back to add any text borders.)

Tables

Tables are an excellent way to display information and, if the borders are removed, can be used as an alternative way to create columns of text or numbers.

For example, the Secretary of the Hambledean Allotment Association produced a leaflet on plant infections and displayed the details in table format (see Figure 4.12).

Infection	Plants infected	Chemical name	Form
Galls	Azaleas	Bordeaux mixture	Powder
Peach leaf curl	Ornamental fruits	Lime-sulphur	Powder or suspension
Onion white rot	Onions	Calomel	Powder
Black spot	Roses	Cheshunt compound	Powder or solution
Rusts	Ornamental plants	Mancozeb	Wettable powder

Figure 4.12

To produce a similar table, click the **Insert Table** button and drag the mouse across the number of squares ('cells') that you want in your table (Figure 4.13). Let go and the table will appear in your document. (Alternatively, you can go to **Table – Insert – Table** and enter the number of rows and columns you want.)

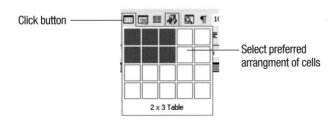

Figure 4.13

Type a heading in the first cell and then press the Tab key (it displays two arrows and is next to the Q key: see page 24) or use the mouse to click another cell. (Pressing Enter will move the cursor to the next line in the same cell.)

To delete a block of cells, click one cell and then go to **Table – Delete – Column/Row**. (If you select text in the table and press the Delete key, you will remove cell contents but leave the blank cells still visible.)

To insert further cells, click a cell, go to **Table – Insert** and pick the appropriate option, such as **Rows Above** or **Columns to the Left** (see Figure 4.14). A quick way to add a further row at the bottom of the table is to click in the last cell and press the Tab key.

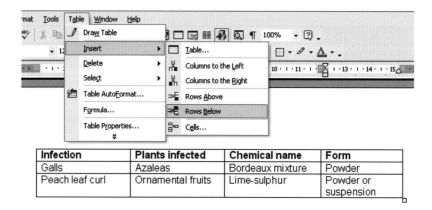

Infection	Plants infected	Chemical name	Form
Galls	Azaleas	Bordeaux mixture	Powder
Peach leaf curl	Ornamental fruits	Lime-sulphur	Powder or suspension

Figure 4.14

Click and drag the four-way arrow that appears in a little box at the top left of the selected table to drag it round the screen, and alter cell measurements by dragging a border when the pointer shows a two-way arrow.

Borders and shading for tables

After creating a basic table, you may want to add borders or shading effects. One way is to apply a ready-formatted design. Right-click the table and select **Table AutoFormat**, scroll down the examples and select a design that you like. You can always change individual features later or deselect some of the format effects by removing the tick in the checkboxes.

As an alternative, select parts or the entire table and apply colours or borders by going to **Format – Borders and Shading** (or right-click and select **Borders and Shading** from the short menu). You can even open a special toolbar – **Tables and Borders** – via the **View – Toolbars** menu. You can remove borders by selecting the **None** or **No border** setting.

Infection	Plants infected	Chemical name	Form
Galls	Azaleas	Bordeaux mixture	Powder
Peach leaf curl	Ornamental fruits	Lime-sulphur	Powder or suspension

Figure 4.15

More advanced features

Once you start creating publications, you may find that you want to use more advanced features. This is the time to move on to a dedicated desktop publishing application – you will be offered galleries of design templates to customise, including business cards, complicated forms, calendars or even origami patterns. There are many packages to choose from, but two that are commonly available at a reasonable price are Serif Page Plus and Microsoft Publisher.

Word publishing activities

Practise:

- setting text in columns
- bordering text
- inserting WordArt
- creating lists
- inserting tables.

Imagine you have been asked to prepare a small booklet containing recipes that will be sold to raise money for a local charity. Think of a simple recipe you know well and then base your practice on that.

1. Create a WordArt object using the title of your recipe and position this centrally at the top of the page.

2. Write a brief description of the dish, centre it under the title and add a paragraph border showing double lines.

3. Centre the heading Ingredients and apply a bold format.

4. Type a list of your ingredients and then set this in two columns by applying a two-column format with a column break after half the items have been entered.

5. Type some instructions as a numbered list. From the **Format** menu, select an alternative style of numbers (eg adding brackets).

6. Add a drawing of your choice.

7. Finally, delete the ingredients and try setting them out again, but this time in a two-column table. Head one column Item and a second column Amount.

8. Save the recipe with an appropriate name.

Getting the most from PowerPoint

When the visual effect of your work is just as important as the content, a presentation package such as Microsoft PowerPoint becomes a valuable tool. You can use PowerPoint to produce professional-looking cards or posters, and you can also accompany talks or lectures with overhead projector slides or even give a slide show on the computer itself.

This chapter explains how to use PowerPoint for:

- posters
- making greetings cards
- giving a talk
- slide shows on the computer.

Starting out in PowerPoint

In PowerPoint your working area is known as a slide, rather than a page, and when it appears it is in Normal view, alongside views of the textual content of the slide (Outline view), thumbnail pictures of the slides (Slide view) and any notes you may write to accompany a talk (see Figure 5.1). Each area can be expanded by dragging the boundary, so you can work more comfortably. If you change views, return to Normal view by clicking the button in the bottom left-hand corner of the slide.

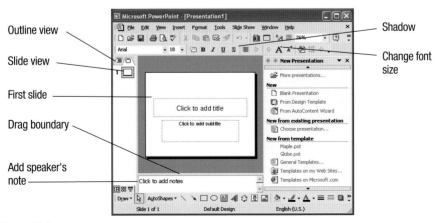

Figure 5.1

Launch PowerPoint by clicking the desktop icon 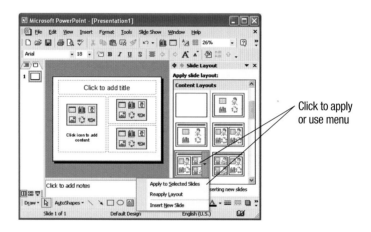 or by locating it on the **Start – All Programs** menu. You are then offered a Title slide layout, but you can choose a different one by right-clicking the slide and selecting **Slide Layout** (also available from the **Format** menu). Scroll through the examples displayed in the Slide Layout pane and click your preferred style. Most layouts offer areas for inserting charts, pictures or columns of text in the form of placeholders, but you can select a completely blank slide or one with just a title and add objects to any layout later. Unwanted 'placeholders' can also be deleted by selecting their border with the mouse and pressing the Delete key.

Figure 5.2

Posters

You saw in previous chapters that you can produce attractive artwork using Word. PowerPoint also has display features that are good for projects aiming for a real visual impact.

When producing any artwork, it is always a good idea to rough out the work on paper first. You will then know if you need to edit the text to balance the effect, where to place objects and whether you need to find some pictures or photos in advance.

Orientation

If you need your poster in upright (portrait) A4 orientation, you will have to change your slide from the default landscape setting. Do this by going to **File – Page Setup** and clicking the correct orientation option.

Text

For an overall title, either click in a text placeholder box if your layout offers this, create a WordArt object (see pages 49–50) or insert a text box (see page 39) and type the text as normal where the cursor is flashing. You will find that the box expands as you add more text, and that you can remove the surrounding border or emphasise it with choices from the **Line Color** and **Fill Color** buttons on the **Drawing** toolbar.

Format the text by selecting it in the box and using the toolbar or **Format – Font** menu options. Extra toolbar buttons that you may like to use include those that increase or decrease the font size in single steps, making it easy to preview any changes $A^\ast\ A^\ast$, and another that adds shadow to selected text $\mathbb{S}$.

If any text box is so big that it interferes with other objects on the slide, click the text to show the border and drag this in with the mouse or move the box to a different part of the slide.

You can continue to add further text boxes until your poster displays all the relevant textual information.

Images and colours

Insert some Clip Art by clicking the **Clip Art** button $\boxed{\textbf{2}}$ and searching the gallery, or add an image from file using the shortcut button $\boxed{\text{▨}}$ or by going to the **Insert – Picture – From File** menu option and browsing through the files on your computer (see Figure 5.3). After it appears, drag the selected image into position or resize it as necessary (see pages 38–39).

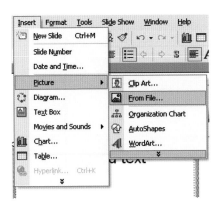

Figure 5.3

One way to brighten up the whole poster is to go to **Format – Background** and choose a colour from the drop-down list (see Figure 5.4a). Click **More Colours** for a full palette, or **Fill Effects** to apply gradients, textures or patterns (see Figure 5.4b).

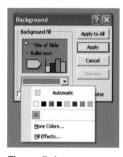

Figure 5.4a

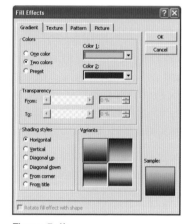

Figure 5.4b

If you want borders and coloured emphasis, you can either change the line or fill colour for a text box or placeholder, or use the rectangle or oval AutoShapes on the toolbar to draw shapes around particular objects. You will probably find that the text or object disappears, but don't worry – either select the **Draw** button on the **Drawing** toolbar and then **Order – Send to Back/Send Behind Text** to show your text or images against a coloured background, or click the **Fill Color** button and select **No Fill** to make the AutoShape transparent.

Figure 5.5

Making greetings cards

A simple card can be produced based on a single A4 sheet of paper folded down and then across, as in Figure 5.6.

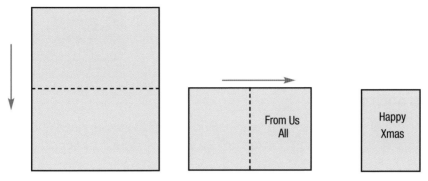

Figure 5.6

In practical terms, to print this properly you will need to create the card by dividing the page into four. The inside message will go in the top left-hand corner, where it needs to be flipped upside down, and the front picture and text will go in the bottom, right-hand corner (see example in Figure 5.7). If you want to, you can also add little pictures or extra text in the empty quarters.

Figure 5.7

Guides

To work in one quarter of the card at a time, make sure that the guidelines are visible. If they are not present, go to the **View** menu, click the **Grid and Guides** option and click in the Guide settings box. These dotted lines won't appear when you print your card, but are very helpful when positioning your designs.

Figure 5.8

Flip and rotate

The front of your card is quite simple. Find a suitable image, insert and resize it together with WordArt or boxed text as you have done for the poster.

To produce text for the inside that won't be upside down in the finished card, first insert it in a text box and format it as normal. Click the box to select it and then drag the green rotate circle round to rotate the box by 180°.

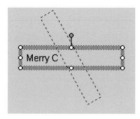

Figure 5.9

Alternatively, select the text box and then click the **Draw** button on the Drawing toolbar and select **Rotate** or **Flip – Flip Vertical**.

If you want extra features on other parts of the card, add them and take care that they face the correct way up before you print your card and make the final folds.

Giving a talk

Everyone gets nervous before giving a talk, but using PowerPoint means that at least your overhead projector slides will look professional. Also, the audience will be looking at your slides rather than you and it should therefore be less stressful than standing all alone on a stage.

Imagine that you have been asked to give a talk to a local community group about letting a property. You might come up with something like the following topics on which you want to speak, and which should therefore be made into slides:

Introduction	**Furnishings**
Finding the right property	**Legal requirements**
Purchasing	**Pitfalls**
Property management	**Conclusion**
Keeping track of money	

New slides

Once you have decided the order in which the topics will be covered, start designing the first slide and then add new slides with appropriate layouts.

With your first slide in front of you on screen, click the **New Slide** button or open the **Slide Layout** pane and, after picking the layout, click the drop-down arrow next to it and select the menu option to insert a new slide. Slide Number 2 will appear and you can go backwards and forwards between the slides by clicking the Previous or Next Slide arrows on the right-hand side of the screen (see Figure 5.10), or pressing the Page Up and Page Down keys. You can also move to a different slide by clicking its number in Outline or Slide view.

Figure 5.10

Lists

Some of the layouts will create bulleted lists automatically when you start typing, but you can turn numbers or bullet points off or on by selecting the list item and clicking the appropriate toolbar button.

You can also create different levels of text in a list by demoting or promoting the list item. For example, instead of the following list:

- Monday
- Tuesday
- Wednesday

You may want to display the information as:

- Monday
- Tuesday
  - Morning
  - Afternoon
- Wednesday

The entries Morning and Afternoon need to be at a lower level than the days of the week. After typing them in their correct position in the list, you must therefore demote them so that they appear as sub-items of Tuesday. Click anywhere in the line and click the appropriate arrow on the toolbar.

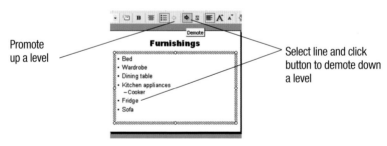

Promote up a level

Select line and click button to demote down a level

Figure 5.11

Using the Masters

To give your slides a 'consistent' feel, you may want to include a logo or WordArt object on every slide. Rather than adding the item to each slide individually, PowerPoint provides an overall template in the form of a Slide Master. If you make changes or add anything to this slide, the change will be visible on every slide throughout the presentation.

To add a picture of a house to every slide, for example, view the Slide Master by clicking **View – Master – Slide Master** (see Figure 5.12). Insert Clip Art or a drawing of a house. You can then make any other changes you want, such as to the font or bullet styles, for example. These will be duplicated on all your slides. Return to your slide either by clicking the **Normal View** button in the bottom left-hand corner, or by clicking the **Close Master View** button.

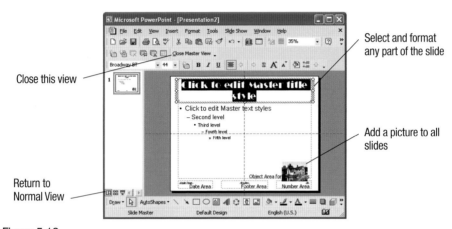

Figure 5.12

Organisation charts

There is an organisation chart option on the drawing toolbar that is often used to display company structures. However, it can be very useful in other contexts too, such as showing any kind of hierarchy or family tree.

To use it for an appropriate slide – such as for a talk on kings and queens, genealogy, plant families, and so on – either apply a slide layout with an organisation chart placeholder that you can click, or click the **Diagram Gallery** toolbar button and select the **Organisation Chart** option.

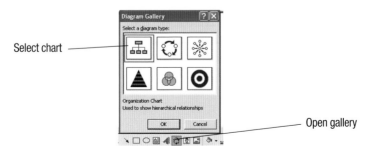

Figure 5.13

67

You will automatically see a basic 'tree' that you can customise in a variety of ways:

- Click any box to add your own text and format using the toolbar buttons, or remove it by pressing the Delete key.

- Click the correct box to attach another alongside or below it in your tree, then click **Insert Shape** and select the appropriate shape (eg one labelled 'co-worker' or 'subordinate') from the toolbar.

- Choose an alternative arrangement of boxes from the **Layout** button on the toolbar.

- Alter box borders or colours by applying alternatives using the **Drawing** toolbar buttons or by double-clicking the chart to open the **Format** menu.

- Change the overall style by selecting an alternative from the AutoFormat Gallery (Figure 5.14).

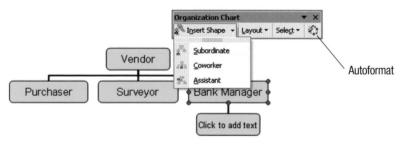

Figure 5.14

Numerical charts

You can add graphs or numerical charts in just the same way. This time, select a suitable slide layout and double-click the placeholder, or go to **Insert – Chart** or click the **Insert Chart** button 📊 , and a basic spreadsheet and chart will appear floating over the slide (see Figure 5.15). (See Chapter 6 for more help with spreadsheets and charts.) Change the data in any of the cells, select an alternative chart type if you prefer, or add colours or borders, and then click outside the chart to return to your slide. To make changes, double-click the chart to display the appropriate toolbars and spreadsheet data again.

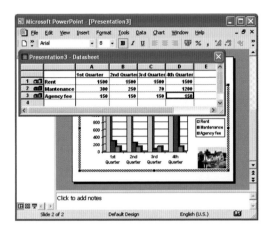

Figure 5.15

Notes for the speaker

To help you as you give your talk, you can create reminders in the form of small thumbnail pictures of your slides accompanied by word-processed notes. Click the appropriate slide and then select **View – Notes Page**, or click in the lower section of the Normal view screen and enter your reminders in the box provided.

Printing options

If you click the **Print** toolbar button, you will print one copy of each of the slides in your presentation. To choose any other option, you need to open the Print dialog box by selecting **File – Print**. In the Print what: box you can now choose to print individual slides, notes pages or the outline of your talk. You can also print two, three or six thumbnail pictures of your slides grouped together on single sheets of paper, to hand out to your audience before or after your talk, by selecting the **Handouts** option.

Colour effects

As different printers react rather differently to the acetate sheets used for overhead projectors, you should check carefully that you are using the appropriate type of sheet before you print. This may mean that you can't use a colour printer. You can check what the presentation looks like in black and white by clicking **View – Color/Grayscale**.

If you do want to use the full colour effects, either for a slide show on the computer or perhaps to print out a version of your presentation in the form of a coloured booklet, or add a light background colour to your slides, you can not only change individual backgrounds and borders (as you did

69

when creating a poster), but also apply complete design templates. There is a range of templates, in the form of combined background colours and designs, that you can apply to all your slides by going to **Format – Slide Design** and selecting the design you like in preview.

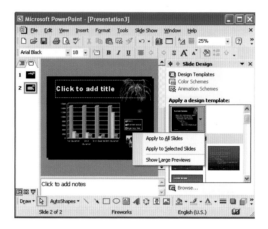

Figure 5.16

Slide shows on the computer

If you have recently attended a public lecture or seminar, it may well have been accompanied by slides, or you may even have seen a 'looped' automatic display appearing on a computer screen in the corner of an exhibition hall.

It is very easy to create a slide show with PowerPoint, but you would need to check that you have an appropriate projector and screen, or large-screen monitor, for it to be visible to all your audience.

There are several advantages to running your slide show on the computer itself:

- The audience will be concentrating on the visual effects and just listening to your voice in the background, so it is excellent for the shy presenter.

- You can make full use of the animation, colour and sound facilities in the package.

- As long as you sort out the timings and slide progression, it is more relaxing than changing slides, as there is no risk of dropping them or getting them out of order.

Views of your presentation

To design and then show your Lettings presentation on the computer, you need to know about two further views that are available as buttons in the bottom, left-hand corner of the screen:

- **Slide Sorter view** displays all the slides at once. It is very useful for rearranging your slide order (just click any slide and drag it to a new position) and for viewing the effect on all your slides of changes to the overall colour or design.

- **Slide Show** removes the toolbars and menus and is the way to preview and then run through the complete presentation. Press the Escape (Esc) key to leave the show early.

Transitions

To start with, each slide will simply replace the previous one during a slide show when you click the mouse or press Page Down or Enter. To make the show more interesting you can choose exactly how each slide will appear.

For example, you may like the idea of a slide appearing slowly from the top or bottom of the screen or revealed as if Venetian blinds have been opened. Open the **Slide Show** menu and select **Slide Transition** to set these transitions from one slide to another. The same or different transitions can be applied to each slide in the show. You can even accompany the transitions with sound effects and set the slides to appear automatically after a certain number of seconds, so that you don't need to operate the mouse or keyboard.

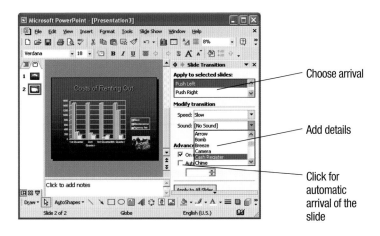

Choose arrival

Add details

Click for automatic arrival of the slide

Figure 5.17

Animations

Even more interesting effects can be achieved if the various items on any one slide are built up during the show itself – for example, words flying in from the corners or images exploding into place, once again accompanied by sound effects. To achieve this, you can open the **Slide Show** menu and apply an **Animation Scheme** to the whole slide, ranging from moderate to exciting effects.

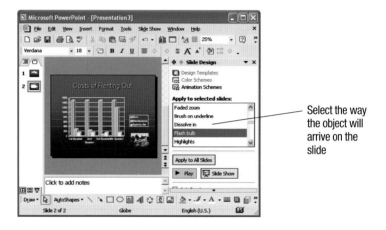

Select the way the object will arrive on the slide

Figure 5.18

If you want more choice, select **Custom Animation** and click any object on the slide before clicking the **Add Effects** button. You can decide how the objects will enter or exit the slide, and in which order. If you don't want to keep running through the entire slide show, you can preview all your changes by clicking **Play**.

Figure 5.19

PowerPoint activities

Practise:

- adding text to a slide
- adding objects to a slide
- inserting new slides
- changing backgrounds
- using the Slide Master
- adding transitions and animations
- running a slide show.

1. Imagine you have been asked to give a short talk, for example, on planting hanging baskets. Open PowerPoint and enter a title on the first slide such as: Getting the Hang of Hanging Baskets.

2. Save the presentation as Hanging Baskets.

3. Emphasise the title by bordering the text box.

4. Add subtitle text, centred on the slide to include your name as the speaker and a venue.

5. Insert a new slide and apply a title, text and content slide layout. Give the slide a title such as: 'Achieving the Best Display'.

6. In the text area, add items as a bulleted list – for example:

   - Choose the right size container

   - Find plants to suit the environment

   - Check eventual sizes to help spacing

   - Colour – contrast or blend?

   - Foliage to add interest.

7. Double-click the ClipArt placeholder and find any plant picture to insert. Resize it to fill that half of the slide.

8. Add a third slide and choose title and two-column layout. Give this slide a title such as: 'Picking the Right Plants'.

9 Set out two columns. In our example, these might be Bulbs and Herbs. You could then add the following bulbs as the left-hand bulleted list: Crocus, Scylla, Cyclamen, Lily, Snowdrop, and herbs as the right-hand bulleted list: Chives, Mint, Marjoram, Thyme, Sage.

10 Remove the bullet points and centre the text for the two headings only.

11 To make changes to fonts and bullets that will be reflected throughout the presentation, you need to go to the Master Slide view.

- Select the title text and apply a different, large font, for example, Matisse or Comic Sans, size 40.

- Select the first level of text and apply a smaller sized, bold font.

- Reformat the bullet points to a different style.

12 Back in Normal view, add some colour to your backgrounds. Either apply a suitable design template (where you will find that some of the changes you have made to fonts and bullets will be overwritten), or choose a colour, texture or pattern from the background fill effects.

13 Introduce transitions between the slides and run the slide show.

14 Animate at least one slide by applying one of the animation schemes and run the show again.

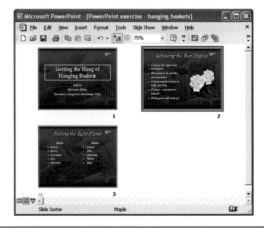

Figure 5.20

Getting the most from Excel

Even if you don't regard yourself as particularly numerate, it is surprising how often you need to perform quite complex calculations. Have you planned a journey using bus or train timetables, for example? Do you check the total before paying your shopping bill or the waitress in a café? Did you work out how much fertiliser you needed to buy for your size of garden or how much foreign money to take on holiday?

Spreadsheet applications such as Microsoft Excel are very straightforward and extremely useful for some of the everyday calculations you may want to make. This chapter introduces the main features of Excel, and concludes with some suggested activities so that you can check your understanding. It looks in particular at:

- creating a spreadsheet
- keeping track of your expenses
- watching your holiday money
- creating a chart
- creating a database.

Creating a spreadsheet

Spreadsheets comprise column or row headings or labels, together with the numerical data – either raw figures or the results of calculations performed within the application. You can use a spreadsheet as a short-term calculator or save the file (known as a **workbook**, consisting of a number of **worksheets**) and keep it for months or years both for reference and to update the figures.

When you open Excel, instead of a plain white screen as in Word, you will see what looks like a sheet of squared paper. Letters and numbers mark the columns and rows of squares, and each square – known as a **cell** – has the address of its column letter and row number (eg B2, C3).

At any time, one cell will have a black border. When you type text or numbers, they will automatically appear in this cell, which is known as the 'active' cell. They will also be visible in the window above your spreadsheet – the **Formula Bar** – and you can click here to edit entries that need correcting (see Figure 6.1).

75

	C3	▼	fx C3	
	A	B	C	D
1	26			
2	34	B2		
3	29		C3	
4	32			
5				

Formula Bar

Figure 6.1

You can move round the sheet very easily using the mouse or keyboard to **activate** different cells and thus enter data in different columns or rows. The main methods for doing this include clicking a cell with the mouse, using the Tab key to move across columns to the right, and using the arrow keys to move in the appropriate direction. Pressing Enter will move down a column a cell at a time.

Once the basic data has been entered, you can change its appearance in a similar way to formatting text in word processing. Click any cell, or select a range of cells with the mouse when the pointer shows a white cross (see Figure 6.2).

	A
1	PAINTER
2	Van Dyke
3	Picasso
4	Rubens
5	Total
6	✛

Figure 6.2

All except the first cell will go blue, but even the white first cell is still selected, as all the selected cells will be contained within a black border.

In Excel, you do need to remember to finish entering data in a cell (by pressing the Enter, Tab or arrow key or by clicking the mouse in another cell) before trying to make any changes. Otherwise the menu options may appear faded and you won't be able to make your selection.

Use the toolbar buttons (eg **B** or <u>U</u>) for a quick method for emboldening or underlining entries or to realign the text or numbers in the cell. When formatting numbers, you can add £ or % symbols or display extra decimal places from the toolbar (Figure 6.3). More detailed options are available by selecting the **Format – Cells** dialog box (Figure 6.4).

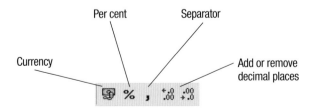

Per cent   Separator

Currency   Add or remove
decimal places

Figure 6.3

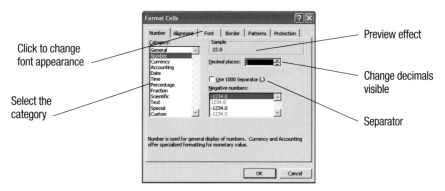

Click to change
font appearance

Select the
category

Preview effect

Change decimals
visible

Separator

Figure 6.4

To make sure that every entry is visible, you may need
to widen columns or alter the height of a row. Move the
mouse pointer over the boundary between the header
letters or row numbers and drag the boundary in or
out when the pointer changes to a two-way arrow, as
shown in Figure 6.5.

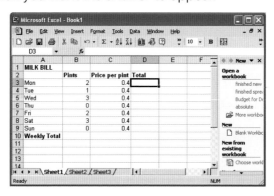

Figure 6.5

Calculations

Once you have entered some data, such as the details of your weekly
milk bill (see Figure 6.6), you can use Excel to carry out various
calculations. To do this, you need to type instructions (a **formula**) into
any cell in which you want the answer to appear.

Figure 6.6

To check your weekly bill, calculating the cost of milk each day involves
multiplying the number of pints by their price and displaying the answers
in cells D3–D9. To find the total for Monday, you would enter the
following formula in cell D3:

=B3*C3

The = symbol is required as it instructs the software to carry out a calculation. You then type the **address** of the cell containing the number of pints followed by the correct **operator** and then the address of the cell containing the cost of each pint.

Excel recognises four operators:

Add +

Subtract –

Multiply *

Divide /

Entering cell addresses rather than the figures themselves means that, if you alter the data, the calculations will be updated automatically, as the formula refers to the contents of the cell at that particular time. If you prefer, you can click each cell as you enter the formula, rather than type the address, and this will be added automatically. However, take care not to click any other cells until you have finished or their addresses will be added into your formula as well.

In the example, when you press Enter, or click the tick in the Formula Bar, the answer 0.8 will appear in the cell. This formula can then be repeated down column D to work out the cost of milk for the other days in the week.

Totals
To produce an overall total for the week, you need to add up all the answers in column D and produce a final result in cell D10 (see Figure 6.7). In this case, if you entered each cell address separately, it would take too long as the formula would need to be written:

=D3+D4+D5+D6+D7+D8+D9

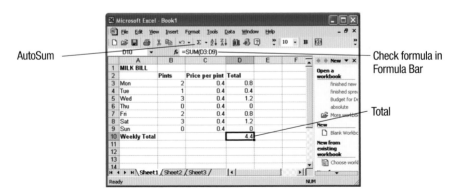

Figure 6.7

Instead, use the quick method to total a number of cells using a special set of instructions built into Excel known as a 'function'. (All the functions are available if you click the **Insert Function** button fx.)

The SUM function to add up entries for all cells in the range D3 to D9 is entered as:

=SUM(D3:D9)

(You can type 'SUM' in upper or lower case but there should be no spaces, and brackets and colon must be entered correctly.) This is interpreted as summing/totalling the contents of the first cell D3 right the way down to the last cell D9 with the colon representing all the cells between these two.

You can even use the **AutoSum** button Σ to enter this function into the cell automatically. Either select all the cells to be totalled first, or simply click in the empty cell at the bottom of the column and then click **AutoSum**.

To check that a formula has been entered correctly, click the cell and look in the Formula Bar. This shows any formula entered into a cell (rather than the result of a calculation) as well as normal text or number entries (see Figure 6.7). To correct a mistake, click in the Formula Bar or double-click the cell and delete/retype entries.

Averages

The AVERAGE function works very like SUM except that it not only adds the figures but then divides the total by the number of items. So, to find the average for a set of figures, you can either use a total already calculated and divide by the number of items, or use the AVERAGE function to work this out for you. This is written =AVERAGE(first cell

	A	B
1	item 1	250
2	item 2	345
3	item 3	287
4	item 4	447
5	item 5	492
6	TOTAL	=SUM(B1:B5)
7	AVERAGE	=B6/5
8	or	
9	AVERAGE	=AVERAGE(B1:B5)

Figure 6.8

in range:last cell in range). You can also enter the function by clicking the drop-down arrow next to the AutoSum button. As well as the AVERAGE function, several others are also available, such as COUNT, MAXIMUM and MINIMUM.

Copying formulae

Copying formulae – or any cell contents – is quick using the mouse. Click on the cell containing the first example of the formula or entry to be copied and then move the mouse over the small black square (the fill handle) showing in the bottom, right-hand corner of the cell. The pointer will now be visible as a black cross +. Click and hold down the mouse button and drag the cross down the column or across the row. All the cells will fill with the appropriate values or entries.

Excel regards dates as special and, if you type 'January', 'Monday' or a single date in one cell and copy this down, you will get a series of months or days.

	A	B	C	D
1	Month	Travel	Papers	Coffee
2	Jan	£26.00	£6.00	£2.00
3	Feb	£14.00	£5.50	£7.00
4	Mar	£7.00	£4.00	£4.00
5	Apr	£44.00	£5.95	£8.00
6	May	£9.00	£3.00	£6.00
7	TOTAL	£100.00		
8				

B7 ▾ f_x =SUM(B2:B6)

Figure 6.9

Inserting or deleting columns and rows

It is very common to have second thoughts after setting up a spreadsheet and to decide to add an extra column or row. To do this, click the header letter to the right, or row number below the new entry, and then use the **Insert** menu.

To add a new column for April in the example (see Figure 6.10), select the column letter E so that the complete column turns blue. Now open the **Insert** menu and click **Columns**. A new column E will slide into place (see Figure 6.11). To insert several columns or rows, select that number of header letters or row numbers before inserting.

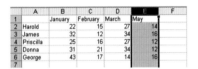

	A	B	C	D	E	F
1		January	February	March	May	
2	Harold	22	15	27	14	
3	James	32	12	34	16	
4	Priscilla	25	16	27	12	
5	Donna	31	21	34	12	
6	George	43	17	14	16	
7						

Figure 6.10

	A	B	C	D	E	F
1		January	February	March		May
2	Harold	22	15	27		14
3	James	32	12	34		16
4	Priscilla	25	16	27		12
5	Donna	31	21	34		12
6	George	43	17	14		16
7						

Figure 6.11

Deleting needs to be carried out via the Edit menu, as selecting the contents and pressing Delete will only empty the cells, not remove the complete column or row. Once again, select the column or row by clicking the header letter or row number and then go to **Edit – Delete**.

Saving spreadsheets

There may be a number of sheets in any one workbook that you can open and use by clicking the relevant sheet tab at the bottom of the screen, and these will be saved automatically when you save the file. However, it is best to open a new workbook every time you want to create a spreadsheet on a different topic, so that its filename will be listed when you search your files in the future.

Save workbooks exactly as you save Word documents – click the **Save** toolbar button 🖫 and choose an appropriate location and name for your file.

Printing spreadsheets

Although spreadsheets comprise hundreds of columns and rows of cells, you will only print the small area in which you have been working. Nevertheless, having created a number of columns, your spreadsheets may be too wide to print onto a single piece of paper. To prevent a small spreadsheet printing onto more than one page, check first in Print Preview. If necessary, use **File – Page Setup – Page** to access the Page Setup dialog box where you can alter the page orientation to Landscape or click **Fit to 1 page**. You can also choose whether or not to print the gridlines by selecting the option on the Sheet tab (see Figure 6.12).

Click here to print 1 page only

Add or remove gridlines

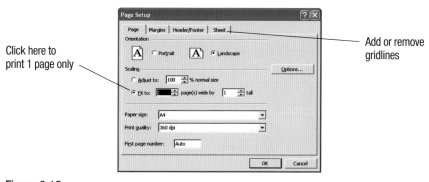

Figure 6.12

Keeping track of your expenses

A spreadsheet can be very useful for displaying everyday income and expenditure clearly and simply; it allows you to see exactly where your money is going. It may seem a tedious task to put all your finances onto a spreadsheet, but once you have created the basic layout, you will find that entering expenditure or details of income becomes almost routine and so useful that you'll wonder why you didn't do it before.

You might want to keep all your finances in one workbook file, using a new sheet each year, or create a new file each time. You could also produce one master copy and then customise it each year, or simply make a copy of last year's spreadsheet, delete the cell entries and then save the headings as a new version for this year.

Formatting a spreadsheet

To give you an idea of the process, Figure 6.13 shows a very simple imaginary budget based on the following items:

Expenditure

- Rent
- Heating
- Telephone
- Clothes
- Petrol
- Council Tax
- Food

Income

- Pensions
- Part-time job
- Interest on savings
- Money made from car boot sales

	A	B	C	D	E	F	G	H	I	J	K	L	M	N
1		Single Person's Budget												
2		Expenditure								Income				
3		Rent	Heating	Telephone	Clothes	Petrol	Council Tax	Food	Total	Pensions	Part-time j	Interest	Car boot s	Total
4	April													
5	May													
6	June													
7	July													
8	August													
9	September													
10	October													
11	November													
12	December													
13	January													
14	February													
15	March													

Figure 6.13

Wrap text

To stop the spreadsheet stretching endlessly across the screen, you may want to restrict the width of the columns. However, some of the headings may be quite wide and still need to be fully displayed. The answer is to *wrap* the text down the column.

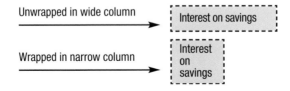

Unwrapped in wide column → Interest on savings

Wrapped in narrow column → Interest on savings

To do this, enter the full text into one cell (where it may appear to spread across other columns), select the cell and then go to **Format – Cells – Alignment**. Click the **Wrap text** check box under **Text control** and the entry should now appear in a deeper cell, wrapped down several lines.

You may still need to amend the column width (eg to prevent words being split) but can keep it far narrower than would otherwise be the case.

Vertical alignment

The header row will now be far deeper, and other headings may only take up one line. To display these attractively, select the cell and, from the **Format – Cells – Alignment** dialog box, align the text vertically at the top, bottom or centre of the cell.

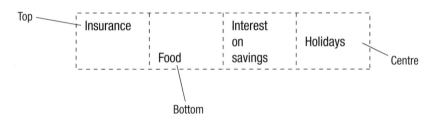

Centred headings

If you want main or subheadings to be centrally placed above the relevant data, you can use the **Merge and Center** toolbar button.

Enter the heading in one cell and then select the cells across the width of the data (see Figure 6.14).

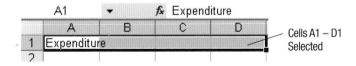

Figure 6.14

Click the **Merge** button and the heading will 'jump' into the centre of the selected cell area. It will look as if the heading is in cell C1, but it is in an enlarged A1 and the next cell is now E1 (see Figure 6.15).

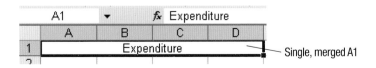

Figure 6.15

83

AutoFormat, borders and shading

For a spreadsheet that you will constantly refer to, it is important that columns and rows are displayed clearly and attractively. A simple method is to realign headings, reformat text to stand out (eg increase the font size and make it bold) and border and shade selected blocks of cells (see Figure 6.16). Either use the toolbar buttons or go to **Format – Cells – Border or Patterns**.

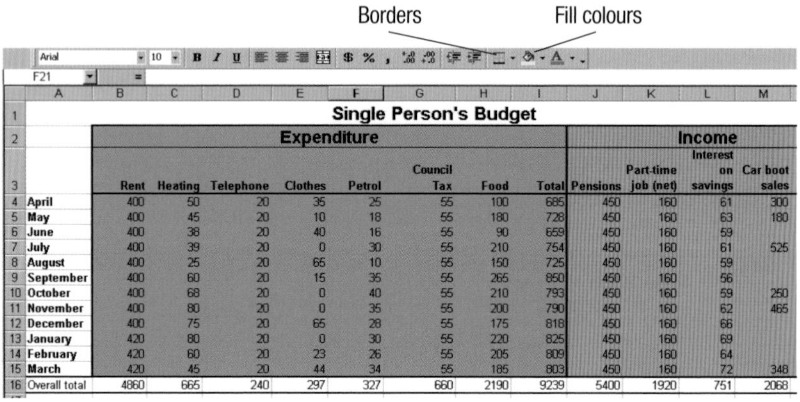

	A	B	C	D	E	F	G	H	I	J	K	L	M
1	Single Person's Budget												
2		Expenditure								Income			
3		Rent	Heating	Telephone	Clothes	Petrol	Council Tax	Food	Total	Pensions	Part-time job (net)	Interest on savings	Car boot sales
4	April	400	50	20	35	25	55	100	685	450	160	61	300
5	May	400	45	20	10	18	55	180	728	450	160	63	180
6	June	400	38	20	40	16	55	90	659	450	160	59	
7	July	400	39	20	0	30	55	210	754	450	160	61	525
8	August	400	25	20	65	10	55	150	725	450	160	59	
9	September	400	60	20	15	35	55	265	850	450	160	56	
10	October	400	68	20	0	40	55	210	793	450	160	59	250
11	November	400	80	20	0	35	55	200	790	450	160	62	465
12	December	400	75	20	65	28	55	175	818	450	160	66	
13	January	420	80	20	0	30	55	220	825	450	160	69	
14	February	420	60	20	23	26	55	205	809	450	160	64	
15	March	420	45	20	44	34	55	185	803	450	160	72	348
16	Overall total	4860	665	240	297	327	660	2190	9239	5400	1920	751	2068

Figure 6.16

An alternative is to choose from one of the ready-made template designs available from the **Format – AutoFormat** menu. Pick a layout and take off any formatting options you don't want applied before clicking OK.

Using the spreadsheet

If you enter all standing orders and regular payments when the spreadsheet is first created, plus the formulae to calculate totals and the difference between income and expenditure, you can keep an eye on the changing totals every time you enter new data. You will therefore be in a better position to say whether you can afford a particular item, or to plan where to cut back if it looks as if you will run out of money before Christmas or some other expensive time. You can also insert extra columns very easily if you find you need further categories, but make sure that your formulae take these new cells into account.

Names and absolute cell addresses

Sometimes, you will want to 'fix' the position of a cell entry in a formula. For example, if you want to work out measurements using a single unit of measure, or find a discount based on a fixed percentage, you can enter the amount in one cell on the spreadsheet and refer to it in all your calculations.

If the cell address is not fixed, when the formula is copied across a row or down a column, Excel's use of relative cell positions will result in errors.

Imagine that you need to multiply all the numbers in column A by 25% (0.25) which has been entered in cell C1. The first formula would be **=A3*C1**. However, when this formula is copied down column B in the normal way, C1 becomes C2, then C3, and so on, instead of remaining C1.

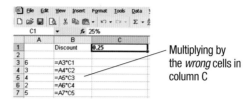

Figure 6.17

There are two different methods for fixing a cell address in a formula: naming cells and absolute cells, as explained below.

Naming cells

Any cell or range of cells on a spreadsheet can be given a name. For example, you could name cell C1 'discount'. This means that all the formulae would now multiply numbers in column A by discount, which would therefore always be cell C1.

To name a cell, select it and then go to **Insert – Name – Define** (see Figure 6.18). Enter your chosen name in the box and click OK (see Figure 6.19). When selected on the sheet, the cell name will show in the box to the left of the Formula Bar.

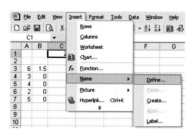

Figure 6.18

Figure 6.19

85

To use the named cell in a formula, either click the cell when entering the formula or type its new name just as you would type the cell address (see Figure 6.20).

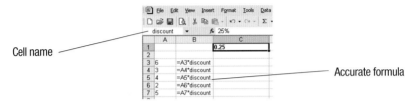

Cell name

Accurate formula

Figure 6.20

Absolute cells

An alternative method is to use the **absolute cell address**. This is done by prefixing the column letter and row number of the cell you want to **fix** in the first formula with $ symbols. When the formula is copied down the column, Excel recognises these symbols and this cell address remains fixed.

You can type the $ symbols as you enter the formula or type the formula normally first. Then, click between column letter and row number of the cell showing in the Formula Bar and press the function key F4.

One use for absolute cell addresses is to help keep an eye on your foreign currency before going on holiday. If you set up a spreadsheet displaying a range of £ quantities and today's exchange rate as shown in red in Figure 6.21, £1 in euros can be found by entering the formula **=A5/ B1** in cell B5.

To fix the address of B1 in the formula, add the $ symbols and then copy the formula down column B to work out all the other entries.

After pressing F4

Figure 6.21

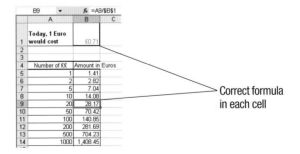

Correct formula
in each cell

Figure 6.22

Projections

As formulae in Excel relate to the contents of a cell at any one time, changing this will automatically update the calculation. This can be very useful when checking 'what would happen if …'

In the above example, whenever the exchange rate changes, all you need do is change the entry in B1 to see what effect this will have on your holiday money.

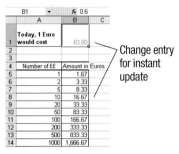

Figure 6.23

Creating a chart

It can often be easier to 'read' charts and graphs than figures, and can be very helpful for sharing information if you produce a pictorial view of your data.

Imagine you want a pictorial view of your standing orders. First, enter this information into an Excel spreadsheet. To produce a chart, select the cells, including any headings, and click the **Chart** toolbar button 📊. You will now be taken through four steps to create your chart. Either click **Next** to move on or **Back** to amend any actions. (Once charts are familiar to you, you can create one quickly by selecting the data and pressing function key F11.)

1. Select the chart type (eg Column or Bar) and click the preview button to check its overall look.

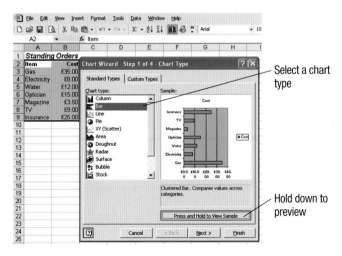

Figure 6.24

2 Check that the correct data has been included and that the headings you want along the bottom or side (ie X axis) are displayed.

3 Add titles for main chart and axes, and if you don't want the legend (key), click the Legend tab and deselect **Show Legend**. For pie charts, you may want to add data labels, such as values or percentages, to the data (coloured segments).

Complete boxes ———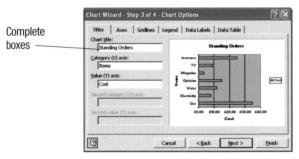

Figure 6.25

4 You can choose to display the chart on the same sheet as the data or separately on its own sheet. The finished chart will appear on screen, or on a new sheet labelled Chart 1. Your data will remain on Sheet 1 if you need to refer to it again.

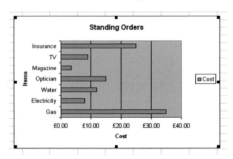

Figure 6.26

You often need to resize a chart to show all the labels clearly – just click and drag any border over a sizing handle. You can also select any part (such as the chart area, titles or legend) to reformat, delete or colour. Either right-click to produce a short menu, double-click or click the appropriate toolbar button or menu option. If any titles are missing, right-click the empty chart area or open the **Chart** menu and select **Chart Options** to return to step 3 of the chart wizard.

88

Drag title

Change font

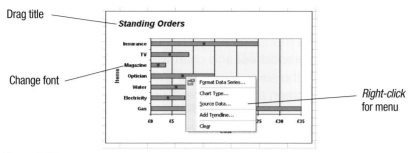

Right-click
for menu

Figure 6.27

Some of the axes may be clearer if realigned. Open the **Format – Axis – Alignment** dialog box and drag the red diamond in the orientation box round to a new position.

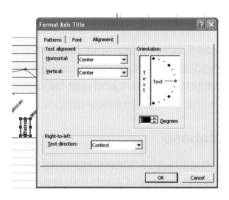

Figure 6.28

One of the most difficult things to decide is what is the best chart type for your needs. Running through the different types can help you decide (see also Figure 6.24 on page 87).

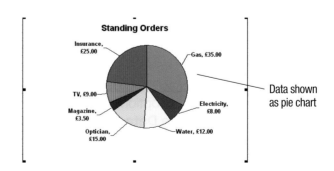

Data shown
as pie chart

Figure 6.29

89

Using the asterisk ***** symbol to represent any missing characters, and maths symbols for more than **>** or less than **<**, you could search for any items that have T at the beginning of the title and a price that is less than £6 (for example). (Don't type the £ symbol in the box, just use simple numbers.)

Using filters

To display more than one record at a time as a result of a search, select the headings and database entries and then go to **Data – Filter – AutoFilter**. You will see small boxes appear next to each heading that, when clicked, display all the entries in that particular field (see Figure 6.33).

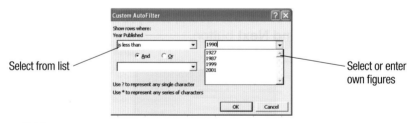

Figure 6.33

To search for all records matching one entry, click an example in the appropriate field.

To enter your own criteria, click the **(Custom ...)** entry for a chosen field. You can now select a logical statement and choose a definite match or enter your own choice in the main window (see Figure 6.34).

Select from list

Select or enter own figures

Figure 6.34

To display all the records again, go to **Data – Filter – Show All** or click **(All)** in the field list.

Excel activities

Practise:

- creating a spreadsheet
- amending spreadsheet entries
- performing calculations
- copying cell contents
- formatting a spreadsheet
- inserting or deleting columns and rows
- creating a chart
- formatting a chart
- printing charts or spreadsheets
- working with databases.

Spreadsheets

1. Try using Excel to work out how much it would cost to carpet a house. Open Excel and enter the following data in cells A1– E5. Widen the columns to display all entries fully and save the file as Carpets.

Room	Area (sq m)	Carpet Price (per sq m)	Total Cost of Carpet	Final Price
Dining	10.75	20		
Bed 1	12.5	9		
Bed 2	9.3	11		
Lounge	14.2	16		

2. The Total Cost of Carpet is found by multiplying the Area by the Carpet Price. Work out the total cost for the Dining Room.

3. Copy the formula down the column to work out total costs for all the other rooms.

4. Now make the following amendments: the area of the Lounge is 16.38 sq m and the cost of the carpet for Bedroom 2 is £14.75 per sq m.

5. Right-align all column headings except Room, and format them all to bold, size 12 in Times New Roman font.

6. Format the entries for Carpet Price and Total Cost of Carpet to currency with two decimal places and the Area entries to display two decimal places.

7. There is no title for the spreadsheet: insert a new row 1 and add the title 'Carpets' in your chosen font type, size 14.

8. You have left out the Conservatory. Insert a new row for this room below Dining Room and add the following details: Area – 13.6 sq m, Cost of Carpet – £24 per sq m. Work out the Total Cost of Carpet for this room and, if necessary, update any formatting.

9. Before you can find out the Final Price, you need to take account of the discounts available on the carpets. Insert a new column between Total Cost of Carpet and Final Price headed Discount and enter the following details:

   a. Dining Room – 3%

   b. Conservatory – 12%

   c. Bedroom 1 – 15%

   d. Bedroom 2 – 25%

   e. Lounge – 8%

10. Format the discounts to show no decimal places.

11. The final price of each carpet will be:

   Total Cost – (Discount × Total Cost)

   Work this out for the Dining Room and then copy the formula down the column to work out final prices for all the rooms.

12. Final prices should be formatted to currency.

13. Add a new row headed 'Overall Total' and sum the final prices of all the carpets to enter an overall total at the bottom of the Final Price column.

14 Add a further row headed 'Average' and work out the average final price for the carpets. (Either use the AVERAGE function or divide the total by the number of rooms.)

15 Ensure all columns are wide enough to display the data and that the formatting is consistent.

16 Centre the title across the width of the spreadsheet and wrap column headings to keep the columns narrow.

17 Print one copy of the final spreadsheet.

F3		f_x =D3-(D3*E3)				
	A	B	C	D	E	F
1			CARPETS			
2	Room	Area (sq m)	Carpet price (per sq m)	Total Cost of Carpet	Discount	Final Price
3	Dining	10.75	£ 20.00	£ 215.00	3%	£ 208.55
4	Conservatory	13.60	£ 24.00	£ 326.40	12%	£ 287.23
5	Bed 1	12.50	£ 9.00	£ 112.50	15%	£ 95.63
6	Bed 2	9.30	£ 14.75	£ 137.18	25%	£ 102.88
7	Lounge	16.38	£ 16.00	£ 262.08	8%	£ 241.11
8	Overall Total					£ 935.40
9	Average					£ 187.08
10						

Figure 6.35

Charts

1 You want to display the carpet costs as a chart. Select only the Room and Final Price data for the five rooms (by holding Ctrl as you select the second column), and create a column chart on the same sheet as the data.

2 Give the chart the title Carpet Costs and remove the legend.

3 The X-axis should be titled Rooms and the Y-axis should be titled Cost per sq m.

4 Reduce font sizes for the data labels to size 9 and reformat the prices to show no decimal places.

5 Print a copy of the chart without the spreadsheet data.

6 Now change the chart type to a pie chart.

7 Add a legend.

8 Add data labels showing the values and percentages from the **Chart – Chart Options** menu.

95

9   Increase the chart area by dragging it outwards and reduce the font size for the data labels so that these are clear.

10   Increase the font size of the title, make it bold and move it to below the chart.

11   Print a copy of the amended chart.

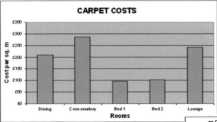

Figure 6.36

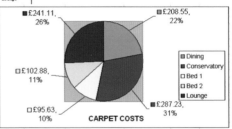

Figure 6.37

Databases

1   To find out if any of the carpets cost less than £17, select all the basic data for the five rooms and go to **Data – Filter – AutoFilter**.

2   Click the drop-down arrow in the Carpet Price box and select **Custom ....**

3   Select 'less than' in the left-hand box and type '17' in the right-hand box.

4   Click **OK** and you should see three records.

5   Take off the filter to show all the records, and then save and close the file.

	A	B	C	D	E	F
1			CARPETS			
			Carpet price	Total Cost of		
2	Room	Area (sq m)	(per sq m)	Carp	Discou	Final Pri
5	Bed 1	12.50	£ 9.00	£ 112.50	15%	£ 95.63
6	Bed 2	9.30	£ 14.75	£ 137.18	25%	£ 102.88
7	Lounge	16.38	£ 16.00	£ 262.08	8%	£ 241.11
10						

Figure 6.38

Getting the most from the internet

We are all used to the fact that we can talk to people in other countries on the telephone, as long as they have access to the international telephone system. The internet is very similar as it is the name for networks of computers that can communicate with one another. At the present time, most computers are connected to the internet via the telephone cable system, but in the future it may be more common to connect via mobile phones, televisions or satellites.

There are two main uses for the internet – sending and receiving electronic messages (emails), which will be covered in Chapter 9, and viewing documents displaying text, pictures, video clips or sound. These multimedia documents make up the world wide web (referred to as the web or www) and so the pages are known as web pages.

This chapter looks at:

- connecting to the internet
- searching the internet
- bookmarking favourite web pages
- saving and printing web pages
- downloading programs.

Connecting to the internet

In order to send or receive information via the internet, you need three things:

1 **Internet Service Provider (ISP)**: you register with this company and it then provides the programs and facilities to enable you to send and receive emails and view web documents. It may also offer space on its computer for your own small web page. Examples of ISPs include O2, Sky, AOL, Virgin, BT and Tiscali.

2 **Browser**: this is the software installed on your computer that displays web documents. Common browsers include Mozilla Firefox, Opera and Internet Explorer and one of these may already be installed, or will be provided free by your ISP. (The examples in this book relate to Microsoft's Internet Explorer.)

97

3 **_Modem_**: the hardware inside, or attached to, your computer that enables computerised data to be sent down telephone lines. Most computers on sale today will already have a modem installed.

Types of Connection

If you only want to use the internet sparingly, it may be cheaper to have a **dial-up service**, which uses the same line as your telephone service (this means you can only use one or the other at a time). This is a less common option nowadays but it may be worth considering.

ISPs offer two different kinds of dial-up service: some ask you to pay a monthly fee and then provide several hours of free connection to the internet each month. Others give you free registration and software, but you have to pay a local telephone charge every time you connect and go 'online'. Choosing the best option depends on how many hours a month you think you are likely to spend browsing the web for information but you can always change your ISP if your first choice isn't right for you.

For anyone serious about viewing or saving films, pictures, radio or TV programmes or spending hours looking for information, it is best to pay for 'always on' **broadband** – this is an increasingly popular option. For an annual or 18-month contract costing about £15 to £20 per month for unlimited use (or far cheaper if you accept a limit on how many pages you can access), you will receive the hardware required to receive the service and can be on the internet and still receive telephone calls in the normal way.

ISPs are everywhere – building societies, bookshops, supermarkets and other large retailers offer the CD-ROMs in their stores that you need to get connected, or you will find disks on the front covers of computer magazines or even sent out via direct mail. Registering is quite easy if you insert the CD-ROM into your (D:) drive and follow the on-screen instructions. You will be asked for an identifying name – your **_username_** or **_ID_** – and a **_password_** that, for security purposes, will be displayed as a row of asterisks (******). (On your own computer, you will be able to set the machine to remember these automatically so that you won't need to enter them every time you connect to the internet.)

One decision to make before you register is how you would like your name displayed in your email address. Sometimes your username will have to be two names separated by a dot (eg John.Mitchell), or you might be able to choose jmitchell, John_Mitchell or even simply John. If you have a common name, you may be told that someone else already has your chosen combination of names in their address, and you may be offered the rather annoying option of mixed names and numbers (eg John.Mitch24). For this reason, it is worth noting down a few more acceptable (and memorable) alternatives that you can fall back on before you start the registration process. (See Chapter 9 for more details about using the email system.)

Once you have registered for broadband, you can be connected all the time and can simply open the browser or click a button to view web pages or send and receive emails. For dial-up, you will need to double-click the browser or ISP icon and a small window labelled Connect will open. It may show your name and password and the phone number you have been given and you simply click to hear the familiar sound of your machine connecting.

Saving money

For any home computer owners using a dial-up service who do not take out a regular subscription with an ISP, the cost of using the internet is the same as using the phone for a local call. You must get into the habit of disconnecting from the internet every time you finish a session. Close the browser window and click **Disconnect** in the dialog box that will appear or display the option by double-clicking a small computer icon on the taskbar.

There are other things you can do that will also help save money if you are using a dial-up service where you pay as you go:

1. Ask your phone company to give you itemised bills so you can keep an eye on how much you are spending on internet calls.

2. Try to connect at the cheaper rate times (ie evenings and weekends).

3. Add the ISP telephone number you are dialling to any special savings schemes (eg BT's 'Family and Friends').

4. If you come across an interesting article on the web that you want to read, double-click the flashing computer icon visible on your taskbar and click the Disconnect button. When you have finished reading and want to carry on searching, click a *hyperlink* (see page 102) and you should get a Connect dialog box up again.

5. When writing emails (see Chapter 9 for further information), stay offline (ie not connected to the internet) and choose to send each message later. The messages will be collected together in your outgoing mailbox and, when you have finished all your emails, they will be sent in one go when you click the **Send/Receive** button.

Here are some things that **all** users (whether on dial-up or broadband) can do to help save money:

1. Try not to telephone your ISP's help desk too often, as technical support can be very expensive.

2. Use the many comparison websites to keep an eye on prices. If you find a cheaper service provider, it is easy to switch when your current contract ends (see Figure 7.1).

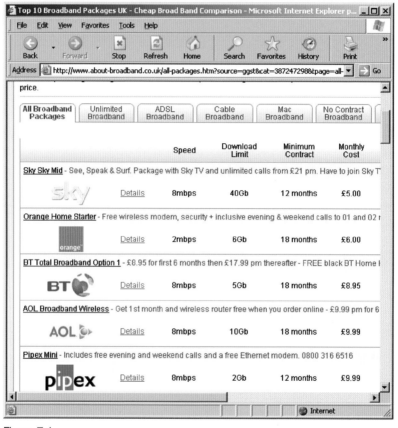

Figure 7.1

Web pages

When you have connected and the browser window opens, you will see familiar menus together with some special toolbar buttons, and in the main part of the screen there will be a web page (see Figure 7.2).

Figure 7.2

Different web pages open (in a process known as 'downloading' where they are temporarily saved onto your computer) as you locate information on the web but every time you launch your browser the same opening page will appear. This is known as your **home page** and is usually a page on your ISP's website.

Most Frequently Used Toolbar Buttons

Back   Click this to return to the previous page
Forward   Reopen the page you returned from
Stop   Halt the downloading of a page
Refresh   Reload the page
Home   Return to your opening home page
Favorites   Shortcuts to selected sites you choose to keep note of
History   A list of sites you have visited in the past
Print   Print a copy of the current page
Address   The address or location of the web page displayed on screen

Hyperlinks

There are two basic methods for opening new web pages: manually changing the address in the Address box or clicking a **hyperlink**. As you move your mouse pointer over a web page, you will see that at various points it changes from an arrow to a hand 🖑. When this happens, you will open a new page if you click the left mouse button. Clickable text or images are known as hyperlinks and are placed in web pages through the use of special code (called HTML) that is written into the page when it is created. The new page will be directly relevant to the hyperlink you clicked and will also contain links to other related pages.

Web page addresses – URLs

Every web page has an address (its **Uniform Resource Locator or URL**) where it is stored and where people surfing or browsing the web can access it (access is the term used for finding and opening a web page on your computer screen). To open any page, all you need to do is enter the URL of the page into the Address box at the top of the browser window and press Enter. The browser logo in the corner of the window will revolve as the page is located, and it will then be downloaded and displayed on your screen.

Fortunately, there is a standard way of addressing pages that can help you to 'guess' the URL and open a page of interest to you. For example, the URL for Age Concern England is:

http://www.ageconcern.org.uk

There are four main parts to the URL:

http://	Means the page follows the code or protocol by which web pages are transferred onto the internet. (In most browsers, you don't need to type this when entering a URL in the Address box.)
www.	Refers to pages on the world wide web
ageconcern.	Is the registered name of the organisation (there is no need to use upper case letters in URLs as they are case insensitive)
org.uk	Shows that it is a UK organisation, such as a charity

Although there are exceptions, the URLs of most British companies end **co.uk** whereas national or local government departments end **gov. uk**. The URLs of most international companies end **.com** (which is why so much is written about 'dot com companies') and educational establishments can be either **ac.uk** (British) or **.edu** (American). New extensions are being added all the time, however, and you may now find URLs ending **.biz** for businesses or **.name** for private individuals.

The name plus extension in any URL is known as the **domain name** and well-known domain names include:

bbc.co.uk

direct.gov.uk (government information service)

microsoft.com

vso.org.uk (Voluntary Service Overseas)

london.ac.uk (London University)

sainsburys.co.uk

So if you wanted to find out opening times at Hamleys store, you might guess correctly that the web address would be **www.** then the name of the store **hamleys.** and then **co.uk** for a British company (ie **www. hamleys.co.uk**).

If you type the most likely URL into the Address box and you get it wrong, you will see a message saying the page could not be found. Try again, altering the registered name slightly and perhaps changing **org. uk** to **co.uk**, or **co.uk** to **.com**. You must also make sure that you have entered the punctuation, such as the dot between words, accurately.

Sometimes you won't be able to open the correct page because the registered name of the organisation is not straightforward (eg the URL for the Automobile Association is **www.theaa.com** not **www.aa.com**, and the British store B & Q has the URL **www.diy.com**). In such cases, you will have to find the URL or the information you are looking for by another route, as described in the next section.

Searching the internet

There are millions of web pages on the internet that might contain useful information. Unless you know the organisation that published the pages and its URL, you will need help in locating relevant websites.

There are three main ways you can locate information:

- gateways
- directories
- search engines

Gateways

These sites contain links to information on a specific theme (eg education, health or the environment). If you open up the gateway page, you can either scroll through the categories and listed sites until you come across those of relevance to your query, or you can enter your search criteria in the box provided.

For example, you may want to find out everything you can on HRT. If you enter the URL **http://www.nhsdirect.nhs.uk/** into the Address box and press Enter, you can click on Health Encyclopaedia in the index. Click the Women's Health category and you will be able to find out all about the therapy and follow up relevant links (see Figure 7.3a, b and c).

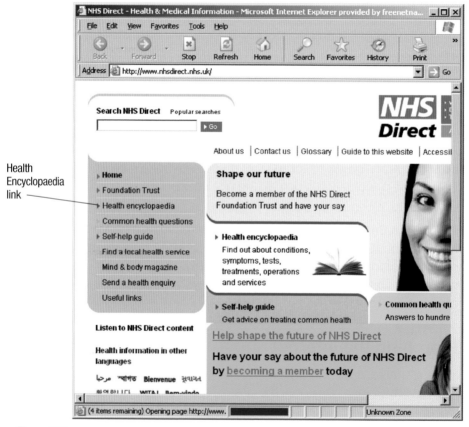

Figure 7.3a

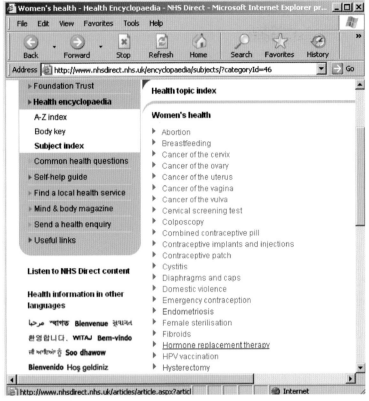

Figure 7.3b Subcategories under Women's Health

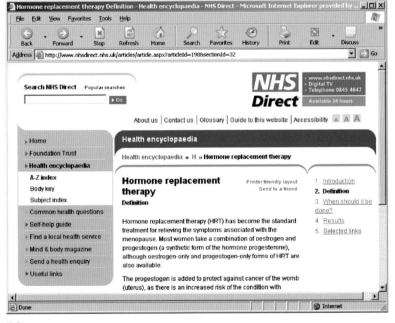

Figure 7.3c

Other gateways you might like to visit include:

- the AstroWeb Astronomy Gateway at **www.ast.cam.ac.uk/astroweb/yp_astronomy.html**

- Intute: Arts and Humanities covering art, design, architecture and media information at **www.intute.ac.uk/artsandhumanities/**

- the Institute of Historical Research gateway at **www.ihrinfo.ac.uk**.

Directories

These sites work by classifying websites under more general categories. Once again, you can work your way down through the headings and subheadings until you reach a restricted number of sites on your topic that have been selected for inclusion by the directory team. As there is no standard method for classifying websites (unlike the Dewey library system, for example), it may be difficult to locate information on a topic if it could come under various headings – for example, would local IT training courses be classified under regional, computers or education? However, for discrete information, directories can provide useful lists of sites that are of manageable length.

For example, to find out more about scrapbooking in the Lycos directory at **directory.lycos.co.uk**, you need to click the Arts & Entertainment link and then work down through the Crafts categories to find a link to Scrapbooking and a number of different sites to visit (see Figure 7.4a and b).

Figure 7.4a

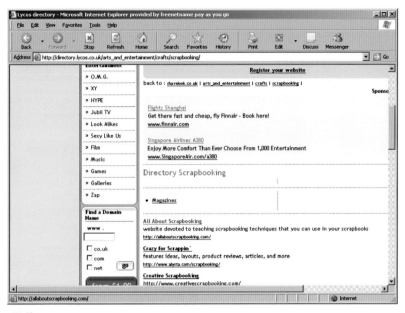

Figure 7.4b

Search engines

The most common method for locating information on the web is to type words or phrases – known as keywords – into the search or query box provided by a website used specifically for searching the web and referred to as a search engine. After entering your words, click the **Find** or **Search** button or press Enter. There is no limit to the relevant sites search engines find, as they are simply looking for an exact match within a huge database of web pages.

In the case of Harley Davidson, for example, entering the words into the query box provided by **www.google.co.uk** resulted in a list of over 25 million sites (see Figure 7.5).

Don't worry if your searches result in a similar number of matches (often referred to as **hits**). The most relevant sites will appear on the first few pages of the list and they are usually arranged ten or so to a page. You should also be able to read a few words taken from the web page, which will help you decide whether or not to click the hyperlink (blue, underlined paragraph title) and download a particular page onto your screen. If you access a site and find the information unhelpful, just click the Back button in your browser window to return to the list.

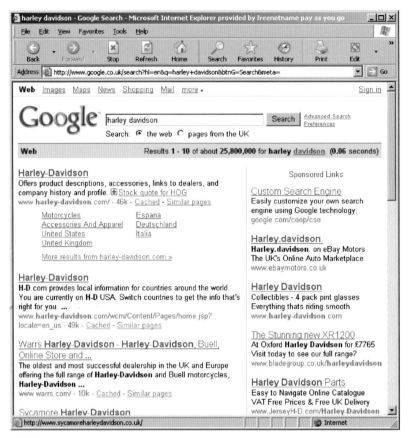

Figure 7.5

Note: many organisations advertise on search engine sites, so take care if clicking a sponsored link such as one shown in the right-hand column on Google (see Figure 7.5).

Keyword searches

There is quite an art to typing in **keywords** – the more careful you are, the better the list of sites will be. It is often a case of trial and error, but the following general advice may help:

- Put phrases between 'speech marks' to stop words being searched for independently (eg 'dog trainers' rather than dog and trainers, as this could otherwise locate sites about dog breeds and running shoes).

- Add UK (if there isn't a country checkbox you can click) if you want to limit your search (eg for goods and services) to this side of the Atlantic.

- Add + or AND in front of words that must be contained, or – or NOT if they should not. For example Cox's apples –recipes should allow you to find out about the history or growth of this fruit but stop cookery pages being listed.

- If you want a general search, you can use the asterisk (*) symbol to represent a range of letters. For example join* should result in sites mentioning joinery, joints or joining.

- If you aren't sure about the best keywords to use, try typing an actual question, as the search engines usually ignore small words such as the, in, and or where.

Useful sites for carrying out a search

Everyone has their favourite websites that they visit regularly when searching for information. Some of these sites act as both directories and search engines and others, such as Dogpile or Megaspider, search the search engines. You will soon be able to compile your own list of favourites but a few examples are listed below:

www.google.co.uk (currently the most popular search engine)

www.altavista.com

www.excite.co.uk

www.yahoo.com

www.mamma.com

www.megaspider.com

www.lycos.co.uk

Bookmarking favourite web pages

As you search for information and follow up hyperlinks, you will constantly stumble upon excellent web pages that you know you will want to revisit. Rather than trying to remember the full URL, browsers offer a useful filing facility where you **bookmark** your page and can return there with one click of the mouse.

Adding bookmarks

Bookmarked pages are filed in **Favorites** (this is called the **Bookmark** folder if you're using Netscape). A quick way to add the URL of the opened web page is to hold Ctrl and press D. Alternatively, you can click the **Favorites** toolbar button, click **Add to Favorites** and check that the page title has appeared in the Name box (see Figure 7.6). If you find the title too long and unwieldy, click in the box and change the wording. Now select a suitable folder in which to file your bookmarked page, or even create a new folder especially to hold it, and click OK.

Amend
name here

Select
appropriate
folder

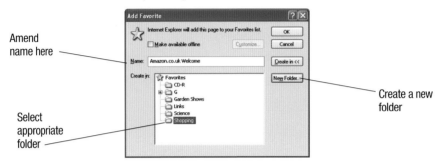

Create a new
folder

Figure 7.6

The next time you want to open the page, click the **Favorites** toolbar button, open the named folder and then click the bookmarked page name.

Organising your bookmarks

To keep your bookmarked pages tidy, you may want to reorganise or rename the pages and folders in your **Favorites** menu. (This is especially true if you have added a page to the Favorites folder using Ctrl plus D, as it will just have been tagged on the end of the list of folders.)

To do this, click the **Favorites** button and then select **Organize Favorites** (see Figure 7.7). Locate any web page or folder you want to delete or rename, and click the appropriate button. To move a bookmarked page to a different folder, select it in the window and click **Move to Folder**. You can then find the correct folder to click in the Browse for Folder window that appears.

Click appropriate
button

Open folder to find
your page

Select the page you
want to organise

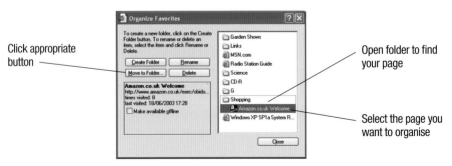

Figure 7.7

You can also organise favourites on screen. Either drag pages to a new position with the mouse or right-click and select an option such as **Delete** or **Rename** from the menu (see Figure 7.8).

Right-click page  Select appropriate option

Figure 7.8

Saving and printing web pages

Saving web pages and contents

It is very easy to save a complete web page onto your own computer so that you can read it again, send it as an email attachment or print it out. Just press the **Save** toolbar button 🖫 and you will be offered the usual **Save As** box. You will see that the page will be saved as a web page file – extension **.html** – and it will open up in the browser window when you go to read it another day.

Many of the 'words' on a web page are actually image files. If you want to save these, or more straightforward pictures, drawings or photos, you need to right-click the image and select the **Save Picture As** option. In the Save As box, you will see that the file type is displayed as **.jpeg** or **.gif** (the two common web image file types) and you should leave these as set. You will be able to open up any of these image files in Microsoft Paint (which will probably already be installed on your computer) or a similar graphics application, and you can then print them or copy and paste them into your documents or presentations (as long as no copyright is infringed).

Printing web pages

Printing a web page is also straightforward. Just click the **Print** toolbar button 🖨 or go to **File – Print** and select the pages and copies you want.

However, you should be aware of two things when printing a web page:

1 The length of one web 'page' is difficult to gauge, and is not the same as one standard Word document page (ie an A4 piece of paper). You may therefore find yourself printing out many pages of material you don't actually want. To prevent this happening, you can set the page range to print page 1 and then print pages 2, 3, and so on, if you want the extra detail that has not yet printed.

2 Some web pages are divided into sections (frames) and you need to check which frame(s) will print, to make sure that the information you want is actually going to print out. Usually, if you first click the section of interest, it will be selected to print alone unless you click the **Options** tab and change the settings in the Print box (see Figure 7.9).

Click if printing frames

Specify pages

Decide copies

Figure 7.9

Downloading programs

On some occasions, you may be asked if you want to *download* programs. This is the technical term for transferring files from the internet onto your own computer and is perfectly safe if they come from an established website. Often you need the programs before you can make the most of sound or moving images on a web page. They can also replace older versions of software (eg your browser or virus checker) or may be necessary for playing games or to keep your printer or scanner working correctly.

Downloading can take a few minutes or much longer. You will be asked where you want to store the files and then you need to stay online as they are transferred.

Web activities

Practise:

- opening a web page using its URL
- using a search engine to carry out a keyword search
- opening pages using hyperlinks
- navigating web pages using your browser buttons
- bookmarking a web page address
- saving a web page
- saving an image from the web
- printing a web page.

1 To use the world wide web to find a possible item of interest, such as a reasonable-quality digital camera, open your browser, connect to the internet if necessary and visit a search engine site such as **www.google.co.uk**.

2 In the search box, type the phrase 'cheap digital cameras UK' and carry out a search. Note the number of pages found (probably over six million).

3 Some of the sites listed may be shopping comparison sites such as **www.pixmania.co.uk**, **www.kelkoo.co.uk** or **www.pricerunner.co.uk**. Select one of these hyperlinks (or type the URL into the Address box if not listed) and open the page.

4 Use any index, search or maximum price box provided to specify digital cameras 'under £100' and carry out a new search, or simply sort the results by lowest price.

5 A long list of digital cameras will appear.

6 If you wanted a 6 megapixel camera, you would need to find out more technical information on the cameras. Click any of the headings or More buttons to find this information. Follow up just two cameras in this way.

7 A quicker method is to specify 6 megapixels before you search for a camera. Use your Back button to return to the search engine or comparison site and type '6 megapixels' and 'digital camera under £100' in the Keywords box before carrying out a new search.

8 A search like this on kelkoo would reveal about 70 cameras meeting these requirements (see Figure 7.10). Follow up several cameras to see their technical specifications and availability.

9 Choose one camera and bookmark the manufacturer's or retailer's website inside a new folder in your **Favorites** menu named Cameras. Name the page after the camera manufacturer.

10 Save the web page onto your computer (for example, in My Documents).

11 Print one copy of the first page of the website.

12 Save a camera image from the same page onto your computer, naming the file camera picture.

13 Return to the list of search results and follow up and bookmark details of a second camera, saving the page in the Cameras folder.

Figure 7.10

Getting even more from the internet

The exciting thing about the world wide web is that it is expanding and diversifying all the time. If websites on particular areas of interest weren't available a few months ago, they may well have appeared and be accessible today. Unfortunately, this dynamism is also a disadvantage, as established websites can disappear as rapidly as new ones are created. So please bear in mind the fact that sites mentioned in this book may not actually exist by the time you try to visit them.

In this chapter, you will find details of a range of websites that may be of interest to people over 50. However, in the long term the most important task is for you to use search engines, follow up hyperlinks or visit sites that you have heard about or seen mentioned in newspapers or magazines, so that you can build up your own personal list of favourite and useful web pages.

The chapter looks specifically at using the web for:

- shopping
- finding a holiday
- dealing with finance
- learning online
- sharing an interest
- keeping informed
- listening to the radio
- playing music and watching films
- playing games
- sharing photographs
- sites for older surfers.

Shopping

You can buy almost anything on the internet nowadays and online purchases are becoming as commonplace as buying through a mail order catalogue or over the telephone. As long as you take the usual precautions, it should be as safe as high street shopping and is usually much less time-consuming. You won't be able to examine the goods closely, of course, but you should always be able to return them within a specified period if they turn out to be unsuitable.

Finding what you want

Once you have decided what to buy, you need to visit the right site, locate the exact items and then follow the online procedure for placing your order and confirming delivery or postage details. Usually you will select items by adding them to a **basket**, **trolley** or **bag** and will move to the **checkout** when you are ready to pay by credit or debit card.

For own-brand items, or if you prefer to buy from well-known companies such as WHSmith, Sainsbury's and Argos, there will be only one website to visit. However, many items are offered by a number of retailers and buying the cheapest or best quality may require some detective work. You can either use a search engine to locate the range of retailers offering the product, or use a specialist search facility.

For example, if you wanted to buy a book on Urdu poetry, you could visit a number of high street bookshops that have set up websites, such as Blackwell (**bookshop.blackwell.co.uk**), WHSmith (**www.whsmith.co.uk**) or Waterstones (**www.waterstones.com**), or you could access one of the internet booksellers such as Amazon (**www.amazon.co.uk**) or The Book Depository (**www.bookdepository.co.uk**). Alternatively, there is a useful service offered by Book Brain (**www.bookbrain.co.uk**), which carries out a search for you and finds the best bargain:

1 Access the Book Brain site and enter your keywords in the query box.

2 From the books listed, click the one you want to buy.

3 A shortlist of booksellers appears offering the book at the cheapest prices, taking into account delivery charges (which can be very high for a single item).

4 Click on the bookshop name to go to its website.

5 Click the **Add to Basket** button to put the book title in a 'virtual' shopping basket.

6 Click OK to go to a page detailing the delivery charges. At this point, if the cost is too high, you have the option to empty your basket or find another book.

7 Click the **Checkout** button, or similar option, to open a final page where you can complete a form with your details and then confirm the purchase.

Nowadays, most websites ask you to register before you can buy any goods. This entails entering your personal details and setting up a unique username and password once.

In future, whenever you visit the site, just sign in with this identity and you won't have to re-enter all the basic information again.

Security

Before you have to pay for the goods, well-designed sites open a new window that confirms the site is secure (see Figure 8.1). This means that any details provided will be encrypted – that is, converted into code so that no one else can read them – and you can feel comfortable entering your credit or debit card details. If such a security alert is not provided, you may decide to stop at this point and place your order over the telephone or in writing, although these methods are not necessarily safer. Normally, a symbol such as a padlock appears at the bottom of your screen when you are viewing secure pages, and you are told when you are about to leave the area. The URL should also change to **https://**.

Figure 8.1

Some sites send confirmation to you by email but, in case there is a problem, and certainly when the purchase price is very high, it is a good idea to print or save the final page and definitely make a note of any order numbers for future reference.

Before buying something more expensive than a book, or using a site without a high street presence, it is recommended that you also check for contact addresses and telephone numbers and read the small print concerning returns or the complaints procedure.

Auctions

An adventurous way to go shopping for anything from kettles to cars is to take part in an online auction. Sellers place items in the auction, usually with a reserve price, and anyone wanting to buy can put in a bid

117

stating the maximum they will pay. If you are unable to stay online during the auction period, an email or a mobile text message is used to let you know the state of play and whether someone else has placed a higher bid or if the auction has finished and the goods are yours.

Honesty is clearly vital or no one would ever use the auction again, and auction sites such as **www.ebay.co.uk** have a system of feedback where buyers rate the dealings they have had with sellers.

Finding a holiday

In the past, booking a holiday meant collecting heavy brochures from the travel agent, comparing prices, searching for suitable accommodation and then sitting in the travel agent's office while they checked whether your chosen holiday was available on the dates you wanted to travel. Now you can do this and much more on the web.

For anyone wanting a last-minute holiday, there are a number of sites aiming to provide this service, such as **www.lastminute.com** and **www.thefirstresort.com** (see Figure 8.2). You are asked to select a destination, dates and airport, and then you can choose from a list of holidays, booking direct or telephoning the company if you prefer.

Figure 8.2

Sometimes you may want to use the web to read brochures online – just enter the likely company URL in the Address box (eg **www.saga.co.uk**) or visit an organisation such as **www.allholidaybrochures.com** and you can access web pages covering all the normal holiday information as well as links to pages offering details of availability and booking forms.

If you don't mind which company you travel with, but want to visit a particular resort, using a search engine should provide details of possible sites. For example, entering 'Cyprus holidays' results in a long list of tour operators

Before choosing a holiday destination, most of us like to know what there is to see and do. Once again, search engines offer links to sites, such as **www.lonelyplanet.com** or **www.geographia.com**, that provide detailed information about the history, culture, countryside, and food and drink of different countries.

Other resources for the traveller include:

- weather reports (eg at **www.weatheronline.co.uk**)
- route planners (eg at **www.rac.co.uk**)
- travel insurance (eg from **www.go.com** or **www.flexicover.co.uk**).

Dealing with finance

A major revolution resulting from the development of the internet has taken place within financial services. More and more banks have moved business onto the web, and you can now buy and sell shares or invest your money in other ways over the internet.

Banking

Most high street banks and building societies now have websites. There are also new types of bank, such as Egg or Smile, that don't have a high street presence at all but still operate very like conventional banks and may offer good interest rates.

If you get in touch with your bank and it offers an online service that you would like to use, it will send you a username and password or new PIN number and you will be able to access the site and check your balance or pay bills whenever you like.

It can be a slow process, sometimes, as there is great emphasis on log-in procedures. Nowadays, you are also likely to have to use the bank's

PINsentry machines, which slow things down further, but once you start to use the site it should be straightforward to access normal banking services.

As banks deal with money, site security is taken very seriously but always remember that the internet can never guarantee 100% safety for any transaction.

You may also want to make use of the service at **www.billpayment.co.uk** if you have a debit or credit card. You can pay your household bills online rather than going to a bank or paying by post (see Figure 8.3).

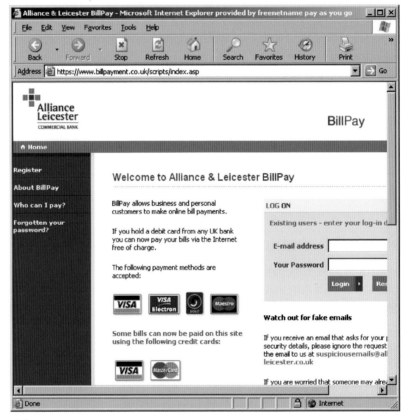

Figure 8.3

Shares

Newcomers to the world of finance should always take professional advice before venturing into online share dealing. You can follow stories in a financial newspaper such as *The Financial Times* at **www.ft.com**, or start by visiting one of the advisory websites such as **www.thisismoney.co.uk** or The Motley Fool at **www.fool.co.uk** (see Figure 8.4).

Figure 8.4

Both sites aim to help newcomers understand internet finances and start share dealing.

At the Motley Fool site, for example, you can read all about banking and investments and join in discussions on a wide range of financial topics.

If you are used to dealing with stockbrokers, or you manage your own portfolio of bonds and investment accounts, the great advantage of the internet is that you can compare prices or monitor the progress of your shares instantaneously, and buying and selling is considerably quicker. As well as the sites already mentioned, there are many online share dealing organisations around and it is worth comparing their services at sites such as **www.about-online-trading.co.uk**.

Learning online

There is no limit to the subjects you can learn about on the internet. Sometimes the instructions are text-based and might be more useful in a book you could carry around with you, but many sites have the advantage of interactive demonstrations, attractive colour pictures and photos and links to related sources of information – and you can always print out copies if you prefer.

121

Short tutorials

Entering the phrase 'watercolour tutorial' into the Google search engine query box, for example, yields a list of over 6,000 sites. In the same way, you can find sites showing you how to do anything from crocheting to speaking Spanish, practising origami, playing bridge, using a digital camera or wiring a plug.

If you always include words such as 'tutorial', 'guides', 'master class' or 'tips' in the query box, you should avoid sites that are only trying to sell you equipment or books on the topic of interest.

As well as using search engines, you may find a more limited, and therefore manageable, list of sites displayed if you follow up category headings on a directory site. Don't follow up the Education heading, however, as this will simply result in lists of colleges and schools. Instead, select the appropriate category (eg Leisure and Recreation, or Computing) and then click subheadings on your area of interest until you can search the list of sites for tutorials. (If you know of a specialist gateway, as explained on pages 104–106, this is likely to be a particularly fruitful starting point when searching for tutorials on a specific topic.)

Some useful tutorial or educational sites that cover a wide range of subjects or offer links to specialist sources of help include:

- **www.about.com**
- **www.free-ed.net**
- **www.thirdage.com/workshops/**
- **www.accessart.org.uk**

Courses

Rather than a self-help tutorial, you may be interested in taking a longer course that could even lead to a diploma or other qualification. More and more educational establishments have now realised that home-based learning appeals to a wide range of adults who haven't the time, or interest, in becoming full-time students, and former correspondence courses are rapidly being transferred onto the internet.

The most well-known UK university to develop distance learning courses is the Open University at **www.open.ac.uk**. It offers a mix of computer, audio and paper delivery of courses, including many, such as those on the subject of IT and digital photography, that are entirely internet-based. Continuing Education departments at other universities, pioneered by Exeter and Oxford, have also put many of their courses onto the internet, as have some exam boards (for example **www.vision2learn.com**), and you can now study almost any subject in this way.

To find out about distance learning courses, either contact the educational establishments direct or search the database of courses held by **www.hotcourses.co.uk** or Learn Direct (**www.learndirect.co.uk**). (For further details of this service see page 147).

Sharing an interest

With a computer in the home, there is no need to feel isolated. People with similar interests are waiting to 'meet' you and have a discussion, or even heated debate, or they may prefer to learn from your expertise or offer you their advice and answer any specific queries.

Social networking sites

Over the last few years, a number of sites have sprung up that encourage people to communicate with each other online. You may well have heard of sites such as Facebook and Bebo, which have become popular over the last couple of years. These types of site were originally accessed almost exclusively by young people but, nowadays, there is no age barrier and groups have sprung up comprised of people of all ages and backgrounds based around universities, businesses, colleges, localities, clubs or simply covering topics of general interest where members set up their own pages detailing information they want to share and then communicate with others by posting comments and queries (see Figure 8.5).

Figure 8.5

Some sites are aimed specifically at older internet visitors and these include Age Concern Community (**www.ageconcern.org.uk/ community**) and the American-based Eons (**www.eons.com**).

Forums and chat rooms

The older more 'staid' online networking sites are called forums or chat rooms, and these are still available throughout the internet. On many of the sites that you visit, you will see labels in the index that refer to forums, chat rooms and message boards. When you access a forum or message board you can read messages that have been sent in on the topic under discussion and, if you follow the instructions, you can add your own comments. One for older surfers is the Laterlife Café (**www.laterlife.com**).

Chat rooms make full use of the internet's interactive facilities – you can have an almost instantaneous exchange of views with people online at the same time simply by typing into the box provided. You usually have to register to enter chat rooms (although this is free and very quick) and provide an identity by which others can address you, but then taking part in the discussion will seem almost as real as speaking directly to other people in the 'room'.

Finding chat rooms is very easy. All you need do is enter your interest area plus 'chat' in any search engine query box.

Newsgroups

Newsgroups are discussion groups where members who share a common interest can exchange ideas via email. Many are perfectly legitimate and informative, but do bear in mind that a lot of different people use the internet and you may not like everything you read (this applies equally to social networking sites and chat rooms).

When people send in their views, referred to as *articles*, these are then posted out to other members of the group and can be answered by anyone who wants to join in. The messages sent to newsgroups are stored on computers known as *news servers* and your ISP usually provides links to one or more. Details of how to join a newsgroup can be found in the next chapter on pages 140–141.

Keeping informed

If you don't mind reading from a computer screen rather than the printed page, you can now get your up-to-date news and comment from the web by visiting the sites of major TV companies or UK and international newspapers and magazines (eg **www.sportinglife.com**, **www. gardenersworld.co.uk** or **www.guardian.co.uk**). In some cases, the complete newspaper or magazine appears to have been published on the web, but most organisations have created online versions that take account of the different format.

Apart from current affairs or specialist articles, there is so much information on the web that a list of worthwhile sites would take a book in itself. Everyone has different interests but here are a few examples to start you off:

- View weather reports on sites such as **www.bbc.co.uk/weather**
- Find maps on sites such as **www.streetmap.co.uk** or **www. ordnancesurvey.co.uk**
- Look up train timetables at **www.nationalrail.co.uk**
- Check spellings at **www.onelook.com**
- Consult the online encyclopaedia Wikipedia at **www.wikipedia.org**
- Find out how things work at **www.howstuffworks.com**
- Discover the address or telephone number of an elusive business by using the online Yellow Pages directory at **www.yell.co.uk**

Printed versions of magazines are now a very helpful way to locate relevant web pages. In copies of any magazine about computers, or covering a special interest such as interior design, cooking, crafts, golf or gardening, you will see website addresses listed alongside articles and advertisements. It's a good idea to start noting these down for when you go online. If the web pages appeal and you find them helpful, add them to your Favorites folders and they will remain easily accessible for future online sessions.

Podcasts

A new way of staying up to date is provided by podcasts – radio programmes (and increasingly videos as well) that can be downloaded and played whenever you want to listen as long as you download the software to play them, such as Apple's iTunes. If you subscribe to a podcast (which is free), future programmes will be sent to your computer on a regular basis until you cancel the subscription, so you need never miss an episode of a favourite programme again.

To receive podcasts, click the logo on any website of your choice or go to a podcasting website such as **www.apple.com/itunes/store/podcasts. html** and browse through the categories of podcasts available.

Playing music and watching films

Thousands of songs and music scores are now available on the internet in a compressed format known as MP3. The MP3 versions will be very close to CD quality and you can play them directly when connected to the internet, or you may prefer to download and store them on your computer or even a portable MP3 player such as the Apple iPod so you can take your music with you when you are away from home.

Most new Windows computers should have the software to play MP3 files, such as Windows Media Player, already installed but, if you haven't got a new computer and you double-click the file and it won't play, you can find free versions of MP3 players, such as WinAmp, on the internet that will download in a few minutes. Links to players are available on the same sites you visit to find music.

A good site to start at is **www.mp3.com**, but you can use any search engine to locate music if you type in the singer or composer's name, the music title and the word 'download'. Once you have located a piece of music you can often click the **Play** button to hear it immediately. To save it to play offline, click the **Download** button and wait for it to be transferred onto your hard disk. Single songs can take just a few minutes, especially with a fast internet connection, but bear in mind you will have to be patient if you want to store a complete symphony.

Figure 8.6

If you want to watch videos, try going to **www.youtube.com** and search the thousands of hours of material that have been provided free by members of the public (see Figure 8.6).

Playing games

Computer games are not all violent or child-orientated, and you can find thousands of free games to download and play, or you can connect to the internet and play online with other people.

You will already have games such as Minesweeper, Solitaire and Hearts installed with Windows. These can be found by opening the **Start – All Programs – Games** menu. To play, open the game and, if necessary, first read the rules by clicking **Help**.

Some of the installed games will require you to connect to the internet to play but it's worth doing this anyway to add to your repertoire.

Figure 8.7

Examples of games sites include **www.funster.com** and **www.pogo. co.uk**. You will need to register but then you can choose your game and download it or play for free (see Figure 8.7). For advice, or to contribute a game or puzzle, you can make use of any forums or enter a games chat room that may be available on the site.

Sharing photos

With so many people switching from 35mm cameras to digital cameras, there is a growing interest in publishing and sharing photographs on the web.

Many sites will let you send your own photos to them (by a simple process known as uploading), or you may just want to browse through the categories of subjects they have stored. One well-known site is **www. flickr.com** where you can add your photos, group them under a chosen theme and discuss any picture you see with others. For easy searching, you add tags to each photo, which act as keywords. There is even a facility to link your photo to a map, if location is relevant to the theme.

Sites for the Over 50s

As well as the Age Concern site (**www.ageconcern.org.uk**), there are a number of other UK sites that have been established specifically for the older internet surfer. They fall into three broad categories: those published by organisations such as charities that are there to provide advice and campaign on behalf of older people; sites with the limited aim of providing hyperlinks to other sources of information; and more entertainment-based sites that offer a mix of magazine-style articles, news, chat rooms or forums, and some advertising of relevant books, equipment, holidays or financial advice, and so on:

- **www.laterlife.co.uk** (magazine-style)
- **www.idf50.co.uk** (standing for 'I don't feel 50' and mainly offering links but with some interest areas such as the music or computer rooms)
- **www.silversurfers.net** (links to related sites)
- **www.retirement-matters.co.uk** (magazine-style)
- **www.helptheaged.org.uk** (charity)
- **www.digitalunite.net** (meeting place and emphasis on computer training).

Every site will offer some links to others on related topics so that half an hour of browsing could result in a huge bank of resources that you can draw on whenever you need help with an issue related to being over 50.

You can find listings of other relevant sites in the Age Concern publication *How to be a Silver Surfer*.

Getting the most from email

Email stands for electronic mail and is the method for sending messages from your computer to another linked through the internet. As you only need to connect when you are sending or receiving messages, it can be a very cheap means of communication for those using a dial-up service, with the telephone call normally lasting just a few seconds.

Unlike a telephone conversation, the people you write to don't need to be anywhere near their computers when you send your message. Messages are stored on a remote computer known as the server and waiting emails are delivered whenever anyone clicks their **Send and Receive** button.

This chapter explains how to use email. It specifically looks at:

- email addresses
- different email systems
- mailboxes and folders
- writing an email
- sending your message
- receiving messages
- sending and receiving attachments
- using an address book
- organising your messages
- participating in newsgroups
- dealing with spam.

Email addresses

An email address consists of a username, the 'at' symbol (@) and then the domain name of the recipient's server. For example:

john.mitchell@virgin.net or **today@bbc.co.uk**

There is no equivalent to the telephone directory and so finding someone's email address can be difficult. If you cannot contact them by other means to get their correct address, you can try using the people-finding directories accessed via the **Find – People** option in your email system, but this is very much a hit and miss option.

As with everything on the internet, the exact address must be typed accurately. If it is not, you will soon get a message from the administrator of the service saying that the email was not delivered.

Different email systems

There are two basic systems you could use: software installed on your own computer (such as Outlook Express, Eudora or some ISP-customised systems that should all be available for you to use offline for most of the time); or a free email service offered from a website such as **www.hotmail.com** or **www.yahoo.com** that you have to connect to in order to use.

To use a web-based system, you register by going to the website and filling in a short questionnaire to include a choice of username and password. Each time you want to read, compose, send or receive messages, you first 'log in' by entering these details.

It is clearly cheaper if you are not on broadband and have a computer at home to use systems such as Outlook Express. You can always register with a web-based service if you are away from home a great deal, or you don't have your own computer and need to access emails in different countries or from different places such as a computer club or internet cafe. (Outlook Express will even allow you to set up an account that offers access to your emails from different computers. You can find out how to do this from the Help menu.)

At the present time, the website **www.mail2web.com** is available where you can sign in and check your email for any email address wherever you happen to be. It is useful for deleting large unwanted emails without having to wait for them to download at home.

As the different email systems work in a similar way, this book explains how to use Outlook Express. You should then find it quite simple to use any other system provided by your ISP or web-based service.

Mailboxes and folders

When you first open Outlook Express (see Figure 9.1), you will see a general contents page, including a Tip of the day, and you can open any of the folders in the left-hand pane to view their contents by clicking their name. At the bottom of the main page click the checkbox if you want to set the system to open your incoming mail folder – the Inbox – automatically when Outlook Express starts.

Send or receive messages

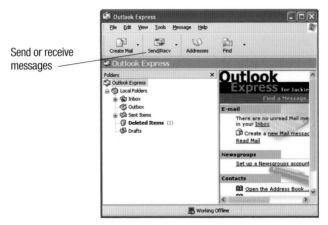

Figure 9.1

For those not on broadband, if the Dial-up Connection box appears, click Work Offline to save paying for reading and thinking time.

The main folders you will open regularly are:

- **Inbox**: all new messages arrive here and will remain until you move or delete them.

- **Outbox**: when you send a message (or select the option to send it later), it will be stored here until you connect to the internet or click **Send**.

- **Sent Items**: this holds copies of any messages that you have sent.

- **Deleted Items**: messages you don't want are stored here until you empty the folder.

- **Drafts**: you can save any messages here, and then send or work on them later, if you select **File – Save** instead of clicking the **Send** button.

Writing an email

If you click the **Create Mail** button (which may be labelled **Compose** or **New** in other systems) you will open a composing window (see Figure 9.2).

Click to send straightaway or as soon as you go online

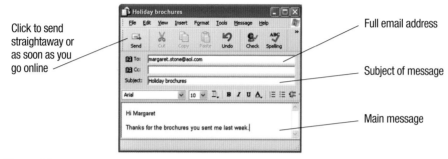

Full email address

Subject of message

Main message

Figure 9.2

There are boxes in which to enter the email addresses of people receiving the original (**To:**) or copies (**Cc:**) of the message, and a Subject: box. Try to type a brief but clear title here that will make someone want to read your message.

You won't need to enter your own email address, as this is included automatically.

In the main window, you can type your message just as you would write a letter, although emails tend to be rather less formal and many people start with 'Hi' or 'Hello' rather than 'Dear …' . You won't need to worry about the look of your message, although you will have a basic formatting toolbar, as most email systems don't support ornate and complex formatting. (To send an attractively word-processed message, it is best to keep it in its original format and send it as an attachment as described on pages 135–137.)

Before you send or store your message, click the **Spelling** button to carry out a quick spelling check, as the cautionary red or green wavy lines you find appearing in Word will not appear in an email message.

Sending your message

Once you have finished writing your message, select **File – Send Later** if you are creating several messages, so that they are all stored temporarily in your outgoing mailbox. Otherwise, click the **Send** button. If you are already connected to the internet, the message will be sent instantly. If not, you will be reminded that you need to connect and the message will be placed, ready, in your Outbox.

When a message disappears from the Outbox and can be found in your **Sent** folder, and you do not receive any error messages soon afterwards, you can assume that it has reached the correct server – although you won't know if or when it arrives in someone's Inbox until you receive a reply.

Receiving messages

To see if any messages have arrived for you since you last checked, you need to be connected to the internet and click the **Send and Receive** button on the main toolbar. If there are any messages for you, you will see a number appear next to the Inbox folder showing new, unread messages, and there will be a message at the bottom of the screen saying how many messages have arrived.

Opening the Inbox (see Figure 9.3) will reveal the messages that have been sent to you. You can see details of the sender together with the subject of the message, and can scroll through the text of any selected messages if a preview pane is displayed. (To add or remove the preview pane, go to **View – Layout** and click the preview checkbox for the option you prefer.) Double-clicking any message will open it fully on screen in its own window.

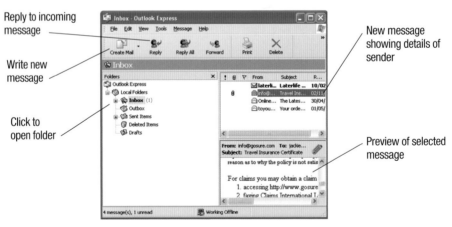

Reply to incoming message

Write new message

Click to open folder

New message showing details of sender

Preview of selected message

Figure 9.3

Replying and forwarding

The quick way to reply to someone is to select the message and click the **Reply** button. You will then see a composing box with their name already entered in the To: box and the subject of their message, preceded by **Re:**, in the Subject box (see Figure 9.4).

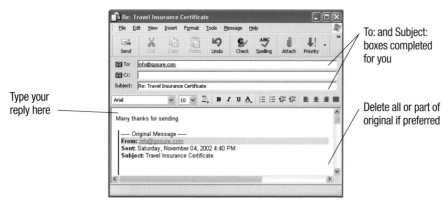

Type your reply here

To: and Subject: boxes completed for you

Delete all or part of original if preferred

Figure 9.4

You can either delete the original message (which shows in the main message window), or leave all or part of it there as a reminder. Add your comments where the cursor is flashing and then treat it just like a normal outgoing email.

The **Reply All** button should only be clicked if you can see from the Cc: box that you are on a mailing list and you want everyone else, as well as the sender of the message, to read your reply.

Forwarding a message to someone else is also easy: click the **Forward** button and add their address in the To: box and your comments on the message in the main window. You will notice that the **Subject**: box is already completed for you and this time contains the original title preceded by **Fw**:.

Sending and receiving attachments

As long as you create and save documents or pictures using commonly available software packages, you should be able to send them as **attachments** to your emails and they should be easy for other people to open and view. Documents created in Word, for example, or saved in a simplified format known as Rich Text Format (.rtf) should be fine. Image files that are commonly used on computers include JPEG (.jpg), GIF (.gif) and Bitmap (.bmp).

The advantage of attaching files is that all the formatting, colours or layouts will be maintained, as the file will open up in an appropriate application when it is received. Attachments are ideal, for example, if you want to send photos of a new baby or a family wedding to relatives and friends overseas. You can do this almost as soon as the event takes place as long as you have a digital camera available.

135

To send your attachment, start composing your new message and then click the Attachment button or go to **Insert – File Attachment** (see Figure 9.5).

Click here

Figure 9.5

You can now look through your files until you find the correct picture, select it and click **Attach** (see Figure 9.6).

Select file

Click to return to message

Figure 9.6

Back in your message, you will see a new box has opened displaying details of the attached file. You can attach further files in the same way before sending the message (see Figure 9.7).

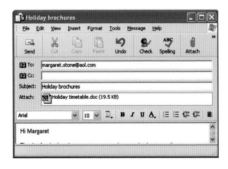

Figure 9.7

When you receive mail, you can tell that a message has an attachment, as it displays a paperclip symbol ✏. To open an attachment, you can either fully open the message and double-click the filename in the Attach box, or you can preview the message and click the paperclip symbol that appears in the corner. This will drop down a list of the attachments and you can select any to open or save (see Figure 9.8).

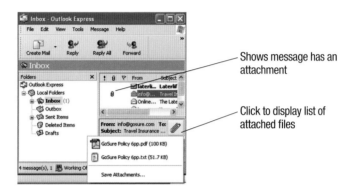

Shows message has an attachment

Click to display list of attached files

Figure 9.8

Compressed files

Many files, especially images, are very large and take a while to send via email. Windows XP offers a quick way to compress them (also known as zipping) so that they take up far less space. In My Documents, right-click one or more files and select **Send to – Compressed (zipped) Folder**. A yellow folder appears (known as an archive) with a zip on it that contains your file(s), and this can then be attached in the same way as any normal file (see Figure 9.9).

Archive

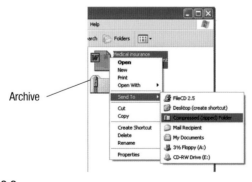

Figure 9.9

When an archive containing compressed files is received, save it onto your computer if directed to do so and double-click to view its contents.

Using an address book

Once you start using emails, you will find there are certain people you write to regularly. As with a normal address book, you can store email addresses; because they are on your computer you will also be able to insert them automatically into your messages.

When you want to add the address of someone who has written to you, find their email in the Inbox, open it and right-click the name in the From box. Select **Add Sender to Address Book**. If you have replied to them before, your system may be set up to add addresses automatically, so that you may get a message to say this has been done. (If you want to set up your system to do this, go to **Tools – Options – Send** and click the box that says **Automatically put people I reply to in my Address Book**.)

Very often, someone new will give you their email address in person or you'll find it on a card or letter. To add their details, click the **Addresses** button, or go to **Tools – Address Book**, to open the Address Book window. Click **New – New Contact**, and complete the name and email boxes (see Figure 9.10). When you click **Add** and OK, the new email address will be added to your Address Book list.

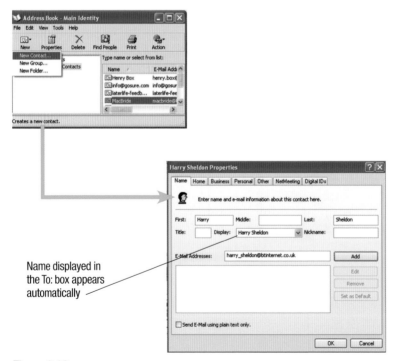

Name displayed in the To: box appears automatically

Figure 9.10

For your next message to someone in your Address Book, click the book symbol next to the To: box in the new message window, find their name and click the To: or Cc: button to add the address to the correct box (see Figure 9.11). Click OK to return to your message.

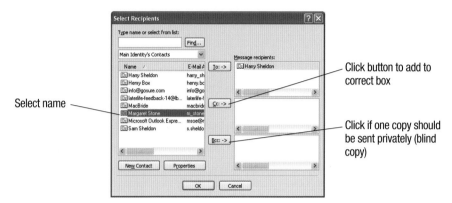

Select name

Click button to add to correct box

Click if one copy should be sent privately (blind copy)

Figure 9.11

You can also start entering an email address in the To: box, as this should bring up the details of people in your Address Book whose names start with the letter(s) you type.

Organising your messages

It is not a good idea to leave all your messages in the Inbox, as you will find it hard to see which emails are new, and even harder to locate an old message when you need to.

Just like file management in Explorer, you can make folders inside your Inbox and keep your messages organised inside them. Do this by right-clicking the Inbox and selecting **New Folder**. Give the folder that appears a meaningful name.

To move messages into your new folders, either drag them (see page 17) across the window from right to left pane, or select each one (or a range/ several individual messages while holding down Shift/Ctrl) and right-click to obtain a **Move to Folder** (or **Copy to Folder**) menu option. Click the correct folder in the window that appears and click OK.

Messages can also be treated like any other files – use the **File** menu options to print copies or save them in suitable folders on your hard disk.

To find your messages, expand the Inbox folders structure by clicking the plus (+) symbol, open the appropriate folder and view its contents in the right pane of the Outlook Express window.

As well as organising messages, it is vital to delete any you are sure you won't want to read again. Just select them and press the Delete key. They will actually be placed in the Deleted Items folder so that, if you make a mistake, you can open the folder and move them out again. Don't forget to right-click and select **Empty Deleted Items folder** or find this option on the **Edit** menu to delete the contents of this folder altogether from time to time.

Participating in newsgroups

As mentioned in Chapter 8, there are thousands of newsgroups devoted to different subject areas and you can take part in their discussions using your email system or through a web-based site such as **www.google. co.uk – Groups**.

Once you have joined your chosen newsgroup(s) you will be sent copies of recent articles. You can choose to reply to just the author of the article or to everyone in the group.

Before posting your first article, it's a good idea to check the advice provided on newsgroup rules (known as *netiquette*) as well as to read any articles entitled FAQs – frequently asked questions. As anyone is free to join a newsgroup, some have *moderators* who check and filter out articles that they regard as unacceptable.

If you want to join your first newsgroup on the topic of current events, for example, first open Outlook Express and click **Set up a Newsgroups account** or go to **Tools – Newsgroups** to link to a news server provided by your ISP and download a list of all the newsgroups held there. (If you don't know the name of the server, try typing 'news' followed by your email domain name; for example, **news.btinternet. co.uk**).

Now if you enter current events in the **Display newsgroups which contain ...** box, you should see a list of all the groups that contain this word and you can choose one or more to join (see Figure 9.12).

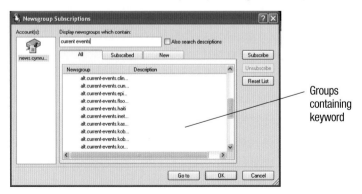

Groups containing keyword

Figure 9.12

To help decide which groups would suit you best, note that they usually belong to a particular category, such as:

- rec (recreational activity groups)
- alt (alternative-style groups)
- sci (scientific groups)
- misc (miscellaneous groups that don't fit into the main categories)
- comp (computing groups)
- uk (relevant to UK-based members).

Before joining, have a look at the messages that are being posted by clicking the **Go to** button. The email news messages will appear in your Outlook Express window for previewing and reading in the same way as normal emails.

News groups are free to join and don't involve any commitment on your part. If you are interested, click the **Subscribe** button (or double-click the newsgroup name). A new newsgroup folder will be opened automatically in Outlook Express and recent articles will be saved there whenever you connect to the news server. If you change your mind, just click the **Unsubscribe** button and the folder will be removed.

Dealing with spam

Before leaving this chapter, you may find it helpful to know how to cut down on the junk mail (spam) that you are likely to receive, especially if you have a web-based email address or you have entered your email address on any unsecured web pages. In Outlook Express, you will find a **Block Sender** option on the **Message** menu so that selected mail in your Inbox can be added to a list of addresses whose future messages will be blocked. (If you make a mistake, select **Tools – Message Rules – Blocked Senders List**, select the target email on the list and then click Remove.)

For other systems, see if you have a similar option, or contact the administrator for advice. In this way you should receive only messages that you want to read.

Email activities

Practise:

- composing an email message
- attaching a file
- sending an email
- replying to a message
- adding an address to your Address Book
- organising messages into folders
- saving attachments
- printing emails.

Imagine a good friend has moved away but you keep in touch and now want to tell him about your new flat. (Either ask someone with a computer to help you with the activity, or send all messages to yourself.)

1. Create a new message addressed to your friend or yourself and give it a subject such as My New Flat.

2. In the main message window, type a message such as:

   Dear Sam

   As you know, I have been planning to move nearer Sally and the twins for some time. Well, I've finally managed it!

   She found me a tiny flat near the shops and the address is 23 Eagle Road.

   I attach a map of the city centre. Please let me know if you can come for the day next Thursday.

   Cheers for now

   Tilly

3. Save any map from the web onto your computer as an image file and then attach it to the message.

4. Send the message. If working with someone else, ask them to send you a reply that includes an attached map.

5. When your friend's message or the copy of the original arrives in your Inbox, reply to it as follows, leaving the original message in place:

    Great news

    I'll meet you at the station at 10:30

    Tilly

6. Add Sam's email address to your Address Book. His name is Sam Sheldon, and the email address is s.sheldon@btinternet.com.

7. Make a new folder in your Inbox named Sam and move in the message you received.

8. Open the message and save the attached map into My Documents or another suitable location on your computer. (As you may have already saved the original file of that name, click **Yes** if asked to replace it or save it to a different location.)

9. Finally, print a copy of the email before deleting the message. (You may also like to delete your reply, Sam's entry in your Address Book and the new folder.)

Figure 9.13

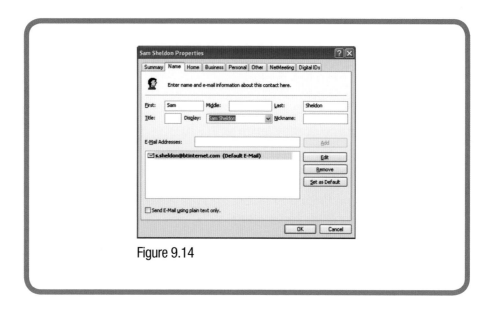

Figure 9.14

Developing your skills further

Now that you have reached this chapter by working through some, or the whole, of this book, you should be feeling quite confident about using your computer. If you are now also asking yourself what the next step might be, this chapter offers some suggestions, including:

- learning through experience
- buying books
- IT training
- CD-ROMs.

Learning through experience

It is only by practising, and learning from your mistakes, that you will make real progress with the computer. Now that you have mastered the basics, you will probably want to find reasons for using your computer so that you can build up your confidence even more and, at the same time, learn new things.

The best way is by slowly moving tasks to the computer that were previously pen and paper activities – for example, you could create a Christmas presents database in Excel or party invitations in Word, help trace a family tree, or learn how to play bridge from an internet site. You will soon find that the computer becomes the obvious place to start any such activity and that it has become indispensable.

Whatever you choose, you will find at some stage that you want to do something that isn't in this book and isn't explained by the **Help** menus. This is where the next option comes in.

Buying books

If you have enjoyed working through this book and would like to move on to something slightly more challenging, covering a wide range of computer skills, a second book also published by Age Concern is now available entitled **_Everyday Computing: Improve your skills in easy steps_**.

Most IT publications concentrate on a single package or activity, such as Word, Excel or using the internet. Although you could buy a book for every eventuality, realistically it is best to spend your money on a book that covers the application you are likely to use most often or a new one that you really want to learn.

When buying computing books, it can be very hard to know which is the best one for you, especially as there are so many being produced all the time, all catering for different tastes. We all learn in different ways and some people learn best from seeing things visually, so they may prefer a book with lots of pictures, whereas others want fuller explanations.

It is a good idea to go to the bookshop with one or two questions in mind that have either not been answered fully enough for you in this introductory book or that are new queries – for example, how do you create your own website, or what exactly is Visual Basic? After looking for the answer in four or five books within your price range – and discarding any that you don't find attractive or easy to use – you will find one that seems to explain things in the clearest way. If it also covers enough new ground for you to feel it has a reasonable shelf life, that's the book to buy.

IT training

No book can answer all your questions fully enough or in the right amount of detail, and there really is no substitute for a personal tutor who can demonstrate how to do something or interpret the written instructions.

You may wish to use your newly learnt computer skills to search the internet to find a course in your area. This is a good practical site giving information on courses throughout the UK (**www.touchlocal.com/nat/ c-468-computer+training**). Some classes are now aimed at particular groups, including the over 50s, but most adult education classes cater for a wide range of ages, and tutors are very sympathetic to new computer users. Now that you have mastered some of the basics, you may have gained enough confidence to join a class, or you may have decided that you can't get any further without one, and you can either study for a qualification or simply enjoy learning more while consolidating your skills.

Courses can be of any length – some will last a few weeks whereas others will take a year – but most of the individual sessions will last 1 to 2 hours at a time, as concentration and stamina fall markedly if you study longer.

When choosing a course, it is very important to talk to the tutor about what you have mastered so far, so that you can pick one at an appropriate level. Some of the basic qualifications that relate to the contents of this book include OCR's New CLAIT (Computer Literacy and Information Technology Stage 1), ITQ or the ECDL (European Computer Driving Licence). If you already had previous computing experience, you will want to find a more advanced course that takes you further with one or more of the packages or covers completely new ground, such as programming or relational databases.

Finding a course shouldn't be too difficult. One place to look is Learn Direct – the governmental information service that can tell you about local courses – at **www.learndirect.co.uk** or on Freephone number 0800 100 900. You can also look at prospectuses online if you go to www.(name of college). ac.uk, or find details of adult education classes in your local library.

There are also less formal computer clubs and taster courses being run for and by older people, and you may find the social atmosphere more attractive than a college. As these groups are not aiming for qualifications or offering an examination-orientated syllabus, you can learn in a more relaxed way and will have more say about what you want to study. The University of the Third Age (U3A), for example, is an organisation made up of people interested in lifelong learning who are no longer in full-time employment and who organise talks, visits and special interest groups in most areas of the UK. They may run a computer club near you and you can find out more from their website at **www.u3a.org.uk** or by telephoning 020 8466 6139. Many local Age Concern offices also offer free IT taster courses, so contact them for further details. More information is available at **www.ageconcern.org.uk/ITforall**

Private training

The convenience of having an expert coming to your home when it suits you, to show you how to use your own computer, can sometimes outweigh the extra cost and may even be cheaper than a course if they only come round once or twice. Costs will vary, but an hour's tuition fee is normally around £20 to £30.

There are tutorial services advertising in local newspapers that will check references for their home tutors, and you can always arrange for someone else to be in the house if you aren't sure you feel comfortable with strangers. One organisation – Digital Unite – has developed a national network of trainers who are particularly experienced with older learners and who must be over 50 themselves. They can be located at **www.digitalunite.net** or by telephone on 0870 241 5091.

CD-ROMs

A wide range of CD-ROMs are now available, either at a small hire charge from public libraries or in many shops where they usually cost between £5 and £40. A browse of the shelves should unearth CDs that show you how to type faster, learn a language, plan your garden, trace your family tree, introduce Feng Shui, draw cartoons or do many, many other things to suit all tastes and interests. Check that your computer has the appropriate memory or operating system and installation should then be a straightforward matter of inserting the CD-ROM and following the leaflet or online instructions.

Now you can see the potential of IT, it is hoped that you will continue to have fun using your computer and will derive great satisfaction from developing your computing skills.

Glossary

Accessing	Finding and opening a web page.
Active cell	The cell showing a black border, in which any data will appear when you type text or numbers. You activate a new cell by clicking in it with the mouse or moving there by pressing the Tab, Enter or arrow keys.
Active window	When more than one window is open at the same time, this is the only window with a blue title bar in which you are able to work.
Application	The named software that is dedicated to a related group of tasks, such as word processing or drawing (eg Microsoft Word or Microsoft Publisher).
Bitmap file	A graphics (picture) file created when using an application such as Microsoft Paint and made up of a collection of coloured dots known as pixels.
Bookmarking	Storing a favourite web page address so that it can be opened again easily.
Browser	The application that allows you to view web pages on the world wide web.
Browsing	(see Surfing)
CD-ROMs	Shiny round disks placed on the slide-out tray in your computer that contain applications, such as encyclopaedias, games, drawing packages or music.
Cells	Squares in tables or spreadsheets where you enter your data.
Central Processing Unit (CPU)	The heart of your computer that controls its main functions.
Chat room	A special kind of website where you can communicate in writing with other people online at the same time.
Clicking	Pressing a button on your mouse to instruct the computer to carry out a particular task.

Clipboard	An area of the computer memory where you temporarily store text or images before moving or copying them to another file or within the same file.
Compressing files	(see Zipping)
Cursor	A flashing black bar that marks the text insertion point.
Database	Information about people or things stored in a systematic way that can be sorted or searched.
Default	Settings for your work or the equipment you are using that are selected automatically and can be accepted or changed manually.
Desktop	The opening screen you see when you turn on your computer. Its name derives from the various little pictures you see that represent items in an office, such as a wastepaper basket (the Recycle Bin).
Dialog box	Small windows (opened via a menu) that offer you various choices to click or type in.
Digital camera	Equipment that creates digital pictures that can be viewed and stored on the computer.
Domain name	Parts of a web address that display an organisation's registered name, location and type of business.
Double-clicking	Clicking the left mouse button twice very fast. It is used as a quick method to open programs or files and can be replaced by selecting the item with one click of the left mouse button and then pressing the Enter key on the keyboard.
Downloading	Transferring files from the internet onto your own computer.
Drive	Slot in the computer housing a disk and usually referred to by letter; for example, the C: drive (for the hard disk) or A: drive (for a floppy disk).
Driver	Software program needed to operate hardware such as printers, modems, graphics cards, scanners and cameras.
Email	Electronic messages sent via the internet.
Fieldname	The heading or category under which information in a database is stored.

File	Piece of work – text, numbers, images or other objects – created and saved onto a computer.
File type/extension	Part of a file name showing the application used to produce it or what type of file it is.
Floppy disk	3½" squares of plastic on which files can be stored. They can be carried around so that files can be reopened on different machines.
Folder	Labelled space where you can store related programs and files.
Font	Type of character used when typing text or numbers.
Formula	Instructions to the computer to carry out a calculation.
Function	Instructions recognised by a spreadsheet application to perform specific calculations.
Function keys	Keys along the top of the keyboard that do not relate to any characters but act as shortcuts to various actions; for example, opening the Help menu (F1) or checking spelling (F7).
Gateway	Website that can be searched for links to other sites on a single theme (eg education, health).
Greyscale	View of a picture that shows shades of grey instead of colours.
Hard disk	Main area within the computer on which programs and files are stored.
Hardware	Parts of the computer you can see and touch.
Help	Demonstrations, explanations and other assistance available when working on your computer.
Hyperlink	Text or pictures that are embedded in web pages and can be clicked to open related pages.
Icons	Small pictures representing programs or shortcuts to common tasks.
Internet	Computers around the world that are linked and can share information.
ISP (Internet Service Provider)	The organisation that supplies software and facilities to allow you to link to the internet and send emails.
IT (Information Technology)	The technical term for using technology to communicate and handle information.

Jpeg file A type of graphics file that is recognised by a browser so that pictures (often photographs) can be displayed on the web. The other common web graphics file format is a gif file.

Junk mail (see Spam)

Justify Text is spread across the page to 'neaten' its appearance on the right-hand margin.

Keywords Any important words or phrases typed into a query/search box that form the basis of a search for relevant records or websites.

Legend Another name for the key to a chart or graph.

Log in Entering your personal name and password to access secure areas on a computer.

Megapixels (see Resolution)

Modem The hardware required to allow digital computer information to travel down standard telephone lines.

Mouse Hardware that allows you to move a pointer on screen and click a button to instruct the computer to carry out a particular task.

MP3 Compressed music files.

Newsgroups Groups of people with a common interest who communicate via email.

Online/offline Connected to/disconnected from the internet.

Operating system Software controlling the general operation of the computer.

Optical Character Recognition (OCR) The technology that allows typewritten material to be scanned into a computer in the form of a word-processed document.

Orientation The setting you select that determines how a page is printed – either upright (portrait), or turned sideways (landscape) so that the longer sides are top and bottom.

Package (see Application)

PC (Personal Computer) The type of computer that sits on your desk at home or work and contains most of the programs and files you use.

Placeholder An area already in place on a PowerPoint slide where you can insert different objects, such as charts or pictures.

Programs	Ordered sets of instructions that the computer carries out.
RAM (Random Access Memory)	The memory your computer uses to open and run the different applications.
Relational database	An application that allows you to search for related data across a number of tables of information.
Resolution	The sharpness of a picture. Resolution is measured in millions of pixels ('dots') known as megapixels.
Scanner	Equipment used to transfer text or images from paper onto computer.
Search engine	A website that holds a vast database of web pages that you search using keywords.
Server	A remote computer in a networked system that houses the network operating system software along with any software applications and data files that need to be shared.
Shareware	Programs or files on the world wide web that are either free or very cheap to use.
Shortcut	A way of carrying out common tasks without needing to go through the menu options. Common shortcuts are available within each application by clicking toolbar buttons at the top of the screen.
Software	The instructions, in the form of programs, that the computer needs to be able to work effectively.
Spam (or junk mail)	Unsolicited emails.
Spreadsheet	Text labels and numerical data created using a program that can perform calculations.
Surfing (or browsing)	Describes the activity of searching the internet for information.
Taskbar	The blue bar along the bottom of the screen that is always available and that houses the Start button, some general information such as the time and date, any minimised files and shortcuts to some of your applications or controls.
Task pane	An optional sidebar that appears within Office XP applications offering shortcuts to related activities.
Template	A file that is used to create a variety of different files based on its contents and style but that is left unaltered.

TFT	The technology used to create computer monitor screens that are thin and flat and take up far less room than normal desktop monitors.
Toolbar	Rows of buttons that act as shortcuts to the more common activities carried out when using your computer. Each toolbar contains a set of buttons related to a particular group of tasks, such as Drawing or Tables.
URL (Uniform Resource Locator)	The address of any web page.
Username	Your identifying name for logging in, or as part of your email address.
Virus	A rogue program that damages your files and is 'caught' via the internet or from infected floppy disks.
Web pages	Documents containing text, pictures, sounds, moving images, and so on, written in code (usually HTML), that are stored on computers around the world and can be viewed when you connect to the internet.
Website	A collection of linked web pages found at the same address and created by a single organisation.
Wizards	Guides found in various Microsoft applications that can help you produce files or objects step by step.
Workbook	The name given to files created in Excel. Each workbook contains a number of sheets that are saved with the file.
World wide web (known as the web or www)	All the multimedia web pages displayed in a browser window when you connect to the internet.
Zipping	Reducing the size of files so that they take up less room and can be sent more easily by email or stored on disk.

Index

About Age Concern

Age Concern is the UK's largest organisation working for and with older people to enable them to make more of life. We are a federation of over 400 independent charities who share the same name, values and standards and believe that later life should be fulfilling, enjoyable and productive.

Age Concern Books

Age Concern publishes a wide range of bestselling books that help thousands of people each year. They provide practical, trusted advice on subjects ranging from pensions and planning for retirement, to using a computer and surfing the internet. Whether you are caring for someone with a health problem or want to know more about your rights to healthcare, we have something for everyone.

Ordering is easy

To order any of our books or request our free catalogue simply choose one of the following options:

- Call us on 0870 44 22 120
- Visit our website at www.ageconcern.org.uk/bookshop
- Email us at sales@ageconcernbooks.co.uk

You can also buy our books from all good bookshops.

Age Concern England
1268 London Road
London
SW16 4ER
Tel: 020 8765 7200
www.ageconcern.org.uk

Age Concern Cymru
Ty John Pathy
Units 13 and 14 Neptune Court
Vanguard Way
Cardiff CF24 5PJ
Tel: 029 2043 1555
www.accymru.org.uk

Age Concern Scotland
Causewayside House
160 Causewayside
Edinburgh EH9 1PP
Tel: 0845 833 0200
www.ageconcernscotland.org.uk

Age Concern Northern Ireland
3 Lower Crescent
Belfast
BT7 1NR
Tel: 028 9024 5729
www.ageconcernni.org